Arranging Flowers

Arranging Flowers

TECHNIQUES OF FLORISTRY

Shirley Monckton

 Sterling Publishing Co., Inc. New York

Published in 1989 by Sterling Publishing Co., Inc.
387 Park Avenue South, New York, N.Y. 10016
Distributed in Canada by Sterling Publishing
c/o Canadian Manda Group, P.O. Box 920, Station U
Toronto, Ontario, Canada M8Z 5P9

First published in the United Kingdom
by Merehurst Press, London, © 1989 Merehurst Limited

ISBN 0-8069-5808-1

Edited by Jane Struthers
Designed by Peartree Design Associates
Photography by Steve Lee, assisted by Cliff Morgan
Typeset by Rowland Phototypesetting Limited,
Bury St Edmunds, Suffolk
Colour separation by Fotographics Limited
London–Hong Kong
Printed in Italy by New Interlitho S.p.A, Milan

ACKNOWLEDGMENTS

It would be impossible to acknowledge everyone
who has helped and worked so hard for the book,
but I extend my thanks to all, and especially Steve
Lee, Cliff Morgan and Barbara Mallard for their
understanding and good humour, and my husband,
Dennis, who so patiently supported the project.

The flowers were arranged by Iris Corrall, Jill
Evans, Barbara Mallard and Shirley Monckton.

The publishers would like to thank the following
for their help and advice:

Diana Beeson of Woodnutt's, 97 Church Road,
Hove, East Sussex BN3 2BA
Jean Graham, All Seasons, West Malling, Kent
Richard Hewlett Gallery, 24 Cale Street,
Chelsea Green, London SW3 3QU
Lizzie Ross and Kate Monckton
Page and Sloman, West Malling, Kent
Mr Smith, Roy and G Hooker, Maidstone, Kent
The Reverend Brian Stevenson, Vicar of the
Church of St Mary the Virgin, West Malling, Kent
Marquee and lining supplied by T Sumner & Co,
Tunbridge Wells, Kent
Oasis is a registered trademark of Smithers Oasis Company

CONTENTS

INTRODUCTION

'. . . a hint or two about simple schemes of colour and grace of line is often enough to sow the good seed in a receptive mind. Then the happiness of handling the flowers and inventing new and beautiful combinations will both bring its own reward . . . and produce the good decoration.' These were the very astute observations that Gertrude Jekyll made over eighty years ago, when she wrote about the skill and delight that can be gained from arranging flowers, and they are just as apt now as they were then.

Although one immediately thinks of Constance Spry and her wonderful contribution to the greater use and understanding of flowers, it was Gertrude Jekyll who pioneered the looser style of arrangement, allowing space to show between the flowers and to make designs more imaginative.

In writing this book, I have tried to make it perform two functions: to present a new dimension to the already-proficient flower arranger, and also to act as a simple guide for the beginner, so that both can derive greater enjoyment from arranging flowers. Flower arranging is an art form, and one that everyone can enjoy.

Shirley Monckton

FOREWORD

This delightfully illustrated and informative book will be welcomed by members of the National Association of Flower Arrangement Societies (NAFAS) and many others who are interested in the twin arts of flower arranging and floristry.

Shirley Monckton's designs and beautiful photographs illustrate clearly the fascinating techniques of floristry and flower arranging, and include a large number of attractive and innovative ideas.

Knowing Shirley as I do, I am very pleased to introduce this book, and am sure that its many readers will gain hours of enjoyment from both reading it and putting into practice its host of clever ideas.

Marjorie Watling
National Chairman, NAFAS

CHAPTER ONE

CONDITIONING FLOWERS AND FOLIAGE

O ver the last thirty years, the use of unusual plants in flower decoration has gathered considerable momentum, with the increased interest in flowers promoted by magazines, books, flower clubs and the media. In turn, the desire for more unusual foliage has been aided by the ever-increasing number of garden centres. One has only to see the thousands who flock to Britain's Chelsea Flower Show every year to realise the universal interest in flowers. There are very few flowers and foliage not obtainable at most times of the year now in most countries, as they can be shipped or flown in from all over the world. Any enthusiastic gardener should also have the skill and knowledge to grow a multitude of interesting varieties of plants that will considerably add to the range of flowers and foliage at their disposal.

However, most arrangers have to buy at least some of their flowers and foliage from a florist. Always choose a good one, because although they can be quite expensive, you will still get value for money. It goes without saying that you must have fresh material, but to the uninitiated that isn't always easy to check. You will not be in favour with your florist if you prod and pull the flowers about, but your eyes, ears and nose should tell you all you need to know.

What to look for
Fresh flowers should be crisp and firm, and foliage should not droop or flag. Perfumed flowers are always at their most fragrant when very young. Tulips and daffodils squeak or rustle when fresh, and the eyes of all-year-round chrysanthemums should be mainly green with just a little fringe of yellow showing. If the eye is completely yellow then the flower is past its best. Flowers belonging to the stock, larkspur and chrysanthemum families should not have been stripped of their foliage (which may indicate that the flower is fading fast and the tell-tale signs have been removed), and if the water smells stale when they are removed from the bucket, you would be wise not to buy them.

Do not be persuaded to buy tired flowers, hoping that you will be able to revive them at home! There are some useful first aid remedies (*see p. 14*), but these are for emergencies only and won't rejuvenate flowers that are close to death. Prevention is better than cure.

Choosing flowers is, of course, a very personal thing, based on your needs of the colourings and types necessary to fit the situation. When buying flowers, you should plan ahead but nevertheless remain adaptable. Your florist will not always have, nor be able to obtain, just the colour or number of blooms you ordered, and substitutes could well be necessary. The most important thing is not to panic! If your florist is reliable they should be able to offer you a suitable alternative, and with a little ingenuity (a skill that develops with flower arranging), you will manage. You will probably also be delighted with the result.

A good, helpful florist is a great joy, and once you have become a devotee of flower arranging, you will find yourself visiting them regularly. The florist should recognise your interest and be ready to assist, but do help them in return by not expecting plenty of attention when they are extremely busy, perhaps when preparing the flowers for a wedding or funeral, and don't expect them to have the complete choice of blooms and foliage at five o'clock on a Saturday afternoon.

I suppose the ideal is to have flowers and foliage to pick from your garden, and certainly foliage is a great boon. There are some excellent books available that will help you choose suitable plants for your own requirements and soil if you are unsure of what to grow. Of course, not everyone has a garden, in which case good plants for the house are readily available and a great asset. Ivies, fatsia, *Begonia rex* and ferns are just some of the indoor plants that will always supply you with a few leaves to use in your arrangements.

Conditioning flowers
Anyone who comes home from the florist and arranges their flowers straightaway will surely be disappointed. Even if the flowers are at their very best, they will be short-lived unless they are conditioned first. Conditioning is very important—there are some flowers that naturally survive

The benefits of proper conditioning of plant material are amply illustrated by this tall pedestal. Assuming that the arrangement is kept topped up with water, the life of these flowers and foliage will have been prolonged, ensuring that they continue to look attractive for as long as possible.

Some flowers will live longer if given the boiling water treatment. Fill an old can or pot with boiling water to a depth of about 2.5cm (1in), and place the material to be conditioned (having first protected it with a cloth or paper) into the water. Wait for just under a minute, then place in cool water for at least two hours.

Singeing stems needs a little care as some of the materials to be conditioned contain a milky fluid that is an irritant. Protecting the flowers with cloth or paper, hold each stem end over a gas flame or lighted match just long enough for it to be sealed. Then give the flowers a long cool or warm drink.

Hammering woody stems ensures they will take up sufficient water for their needs. Some people prefer to clip the stems at a 45° angle, which is fine if only a few stems are needed but when preparing vast quantities it is more convenient and quicker to hammer them.

longer than others, but all benefit from the treatment.

The first thing to do is to clip the ends of each stem at an angle of 45°, then place them in a bucket of cool or tepid water, preferably overnight, but for at least two hours if time is short. Always remove any leaves or buds below the water line.

Most flowers will need no other treatment, but there are exceptions. Plants with woody stems benefit from their ends being hammered before being given a long cool drink. Blossoms such as lilac last longer if most or all of the foliage is first removed. Poppies, euphorbias and similar flowers contain a milky fluid which flows from the stems when cut—dipping them into a little boiling water for 30 seconds will seal the wounds, allowing the flowers to continue taking up water. Roses also benefit from the boiling water treatment, especially if their heads have drooped. When using boiling water always protect the flower heads with a tissue or cloth to prevent scalding. Singeing or burning the ends of such flowers as poppies is equally efficient.

Removing air locks
The reason for this seemingly drastic treatment is to remove the air lock created by the plant during its time out of water: the plant will have sealed the end of its stem to prevent further loss of moisture. The air lock forms behind this seal, so clipping the end removes the seal and air lock and allows the plant to continue taking up water. The hot water will remove some of the air and allow the plant to drink freely. The one real exception to the boiling water treatment is any flower produced from a bulb: long cool drinks fulfil their needs.

Tulips have a will of their own, continuing to grow and move in every direction imaginable even when they have been cut and are part of an arrangement. They also have an alarming habit of flopping very easily. Always buy the firmest and crispest tulips you can find, then trim the stem ends and firmly wrap them in tissue paper or newspaper before placing in cool water for a long drink. Pricking just below each flower head with a darning needle will also help. Some people advocate adding a little

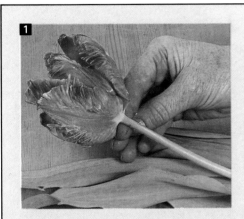 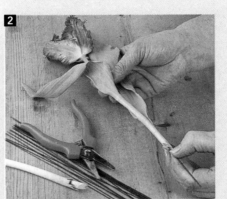

Pricking the stem of a tulip with a fine darning needle, just below the flower head, will help to keep the stem straight and stop it drooping once it has been arranged.

Internal wiring is a useful aid for hyacinths, tulips and the like. Gently thread a stub wire through the stem and into the flower head. You will need a thin stick to support such flowers as amaryllis, delphiniums and hollyhocks; gently feed the stick into the stem until it feels secure.

cold-water starch to the conditioning water, but this is not a foolproof remedy.

Foliage, and such plants as euphorbias, love a bath and enjoy being submerged overnight, or again for the minimum time of two hours. The exceptions are all plants with grey furry leaves—these hate getting wet and will show their displeasure by their bedraggled appearance, which cannot be remedied, by the way. Using the bath for soaking plants is very handy, but it can annoy the family! If so, using an old zinc bath or deep tub will solve this problem.

Some flowers, such as lupins, delphiniums and hollyhocks, have hollow stems. These tend to dry out quickly, after which they will not take up water at all. To rectify this, the stems must be inverted and filled with water, then plugged with cotton wool or soft tissue. Carefully holding the plug in position, replace each flower in the bucket for a long drink in deep water. Sometimes these flowers are very tall, in which case standing on a chair or steps is the only way in which they can be filled.

Other flowers that require extra care are listed on pages 142–3, and I have also included a list of the flowers and foliage that I consider to be of particular value to the arranger.

Pet conditioning remedies

Suggestions for prolonging the life of cut flowers abound, and everyone has their own pet theories. I've heard recommendations of lemonade, sugar, aspirin and even gin, but I'm not convinced that any of these ideas work. If you have conditioned your flowers properly then all should be well. Besides which, it does seem an awful waste of gin!

Often flowers are sent with a packet of proprietary flower food, which I always use, just in case. Checking that the oasis is still damp or the water in the container fresh and topped up, with an occasional spray to the flower heads and foliage, is usually all that is required to keep everything in order.

Prolonging the life of certain flowers

Although not strictly conditioning, there are some helpful ideas that can be used in certain situations. For instance, you may need to keep your flowers for a while before using them. If you are careful, the deterioration of such flowers as roses, tulips and carnations can be delayed for nearly a week. To do this, condition the flowers in the normal way and then seal them in foil or polythene before gently placing them in a refrigerator set at 5.5°C

(41°F). Peonies and gladioli can be left untouched on a cold dry floor for two or three days then, when you wish to use them, you can just cut the stems at an angle and place in tepid water.

Transporting flowers

Travelling with flowers is an art in itself! It is also a very important part of the work of the flower arranger. Some journeys will take several hours, so the large flower boxes are indispensable. These usually have small holes in the sides. The box must be lined with enough thin polythene sheeting to cover the base and sides. Layers of crumpled tissue paper are then placed in the box with the flowers carefully arranged around the tissue so that it supports the flower heads and prevents them moving in the box. The flowers should then be sprayed with a fine mist of water, and covered with a layer of tissue paper and

another of polythene before the box lid is replaced. A word of warning—do not leave the boxes in a closed car in the height of summer, or you will cook the contents!

Emergency measures

Wilted flowers are a particular problem. These can be carefully removed from the arrangement and the original conditioning treatment repeated, before being given a long drink. Sometimes warm to hot water will effect a revival. (A thermos flask of hot water should be part of your equipment.) Occasionally, however, the flower will not respond, in which case you will have no option but to discard it.

Picking fresh flowers

If you are fortunate enough to be able to pick flowers from your garden, it is advisable to do this either early in the morning or late in the evening, because plants are full of moisture at these times. Placing them immediately into a bucket is very good for them, as it reduces the risk of air locks, and sometimes it is beneficial to cut the ends again under the water. When you collect the foliage it will keep well if you place it on a large plastic sheet.

The old-fashioned picking basket looks very romantic but is also practical in that the flowers are protected by being allowed to lie flat. Garden flowers will still need to be conditioned.

Forcing flowers

In spring we are often overwhelmed with blossom and flowers, yet earlier in the colder months we may well yearn for a branch or two of colour. Flowering currant and forsythia are good for forcing. Choose the branches with the fattest buds, split or hammer the stems and scrape away about 5cm (2in) of bark from the end, then place in warm water in a light position. In a week or maybe two, the flowers will be out and you will be delighted.

As one last recommendation, always top up the container with water when you have finished your arrangement, because flowers drink very readily when first arranged. Then give a fine misting of water, and you can look back with pleasure.

The few pieces of equipment needed for conditioning flowers and foliage are just as essential as your mechanics. It is especially important to take them with you when you arrange flowers away from home.

CHAPTER TWO

THE PRINCIPLES OF DESIGN IN FLOWER ARRANGING

Everyone would agree that flowers are very beautiful, but being able to arrange them with confidence and pleasure sometimes requires a little guidance. These are not rules and regulations, for they immediately impose a sense of restriction, but instead some basic principles which will be constructive.

When setting out on any task, one usually has an idea of the finished project, whether it is embroidery, gardening, cooking or anything else, and so it is with flowers. To have a general design in mind before you begin helps greatly to obtain the desired result. The idea cannot be exactly determined as no two flowers are alike and no two pieces of foliage flow in an identical way. Each design is an original, and each creation unique.

The principles of all good design are simple. Proportion is important, relating height, length and depth. Balance is also necessary—a good design always feels right, and doesn't look as though it is about to fall over! Colour is a vital part of arranging flowers and a simple understanding of their combinations and values very worthwhile. Visual interest is part of the whole and the harmony of plants should be satisfying to the eye. The arrangement should also be suitable for its purpose—enhancing its surroundings rather than detracting from them.

Just as a picture has a focal point, so too does a flower arrangement, and there should be a centre to which the eye is immediately drawn. This is the centre of balance, and all the flowers and foliage

MAKING AN INVERTED CRESCENT DESIGN

1 *Choose a shallow vase for this design. Place a block of wet oasis in the base of the vase, then cover it with wire netting and wire it in place by wrapping it around the sides of the vase. The wire will be hidden by the flowers.*

2 *Add the flowers and foliage. Place the shorter material in the centre to keep the overall shape, and choose flowing stems to create the downward curves at the sides.*

3 *Fill in with more flowers. This design is always elegant and allows one to use the minimum of plant material to the maximum effect.*

MAKING A
HORIZONTAL
DESIGN

1 *It is always best to work* in situ. *Assemble the mechanics – here I have placed two pin-holders in the bottom of a low dish, and then taped a block of wet oasis in place with green tape.*

2 *Arrange the basic outline with the foliage. Here, I have extended the length of the arrangement to echo the outline of the dining table, while keeping the top foliage very short.*

3 *Now fill in the outline with the flowers, allowing the outer flowers to trail on the table and hide all the mechanics.*

4 *The elegance of the finished arrangement is accentuated by the formality of the table setting.*

16

should appear to be coming from that point. This gives the comfortable, easy-to-live-with feeling of successful arrangements. If the stems are allowed to cross each other the design will feel awkward and ungainly.

Creating the outline of an arrangement

Every arrangement has an outline, usually made from the finer plant materials or the lighter-coloured flowers. Buds and branches are ideal for the purpose, and it is always best to start with the tallest stem. If you wish to determine the height of the arrangement, you should make the tallest stem about one-and-a-half times the height of the container. It should also be set towards the back of the design, thereby giving the arrangement greater depth. If the tallest stem that you wish to use is curved, then make sure that the tip bends over the focal point.

You usually need five or seven stems to make the outline of a basic shape. Following the first placement, add two secondary stems, in positions of approximately five o'clock and seven-thirty. These should follow the line to the focal point, but not actually end there. A useful tip to help you achieve these important positions is to place them underarm.

The next two pieces should come from the back slightly towards the focal point at ten o'clock and one-thirty, and should be shorter than the tallest stem. It adds greatly to the design if the outline stems are slightly varied in length. If using seven

MAKING A SYMMETRICAL DESIGN

1 *I arranged a smaller block of wet oasis with a larger one behind, taping them into a shallow bowl that in turn fitted the mouth of the pedestal. I then covered them with wire netting that was wired into place.*

2 *Begin to create the basic symmetrical outline with foliage, thereby determining the size and shape of your finished design.*

3 *Now build up the arrangement by adding more foliage and some of the flowers.*

4 *Add the rest of the flowers, taking care to maintain the symmetry of the arrangement without allowing it to look dull or predictable.*

MAKING AN ASYMMETRICAL TRIANGLE

1 *Place a block of wet oasis in a shallow tray, then cover with wire netting and wire it in position.*

2 *Create the basic outline with foliage, making one side longer than the other.*

3 *Build up the asymmetrical shape with a variety of foliages.*

4 *Fill in the shape with the flowers, allowing the flowers in the longest side of the triangle to trail, thereby softening and accentuating the outline of the arrangement.*

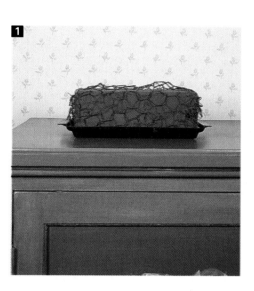

stems as the outline then, coming from the back of the design at nine-thirty and two forty-five, bring your stems in towards the focal point. The largest leaves and flowers, or sometimes the brightest, are normally used as the focal point, and the transitional materials (those which are less heavy), will help the design to blend together happily. Foliage, and perhaps some flowers, must be placed at the back of the arrangement. A particularly important placement, which always creates a sense of stability, is a leaf or bud positioned behind and slightly to one side of the tallest branch, but still aimed at the focal point. This spacial placement must always be shorter than the first stem.

Of course, you do not have to follow these outline ideas to the letter, but they do help to create the right feeling in an arrangement. However, experience will soon make these placements second nature to you. One important point to bear in mind is the shape of the flowers or foliage you are using. For example, if a stem inclines to the right then it is best to use it on the right rather than try to coax it to the left in your arrangement, as it will never look happy. In this simple design try to ensure that the outline stems look natural, and are not sticking out like wings about to take off! You should also particularly notice the depth gained by placing pieces at the back of the design. This takes one's eye through the arrangement, before it comes to rest again at the focal point.

Traditional and modern designs
There are two main types of design. The traditional, using line and mass, and the informal, which includes modern and abstract. The traditional style uses many flowers with rich and varied plant materials. The mass design is often seen when a large eye-catching arrangement is required, although this is not the signal for you to include everything but the kitchen sink! This style should clearly demonstrate the principles of design and the focal point should be especially evident. Mass designs can be frontal or all-around arrangements, the names of which are really self-explanatory.

Linear, or line, designs, fulfil a need for variety and differing shapes for special

MAKING A HOGARTH CURVE DESIGN

1 *Place a block of wet oasis into a vase and tape it in position. Using a tall, simple vase such as the one shown in the photograph will help to create this design more easily.*

2 *Now begin to create the outline. It is very important to use suitable plant material, because choosing stems that have a natural curve will ensure the flowing lines of the finished design.*

3 *Continue to build up the design with foliage and flowers, still following the natural curves of the stems.*

4 *Complete the design by adding a few more flowers until you are pleased with the finished result.*

positions. For example, a horizontal design is ideal for decorating a dining table, when a massed frontal design would not be in keeping at all. The main linear designs are as follows: the triangle (sometimes called the symmetrical triangle); the asymmetrical triangle; the Hogarth curve or S-shape; the crescent; the horizontal and the vertical.

The informal design does not conform to an arrangement in the strictest sense, as it is often composed of just the flowers cut to equal lengths, which are sometimes tied, and then placed in simple containers filled with water. Alternatively, they may be large sculptural leaves and branches placed informally in uncomplicated containers. The modern and abstract designs use plant material more adventurously and conform to the term 'arrangement', using the principles of design. I have often heard these designs described as 'mangled', but I don't agree. In fact, at their best they present a dramatic and often beautiful design, the space within the material combining with the whole to create the finished arrangement. Modern designs feature flowers and foliage in an adventurous way, often using very little plant material at all. Abstract design, more aptly described as structural, is another aspect of modern design that creates strong patterns with the organisation of solids and spaces, and often resembles modern sculptures. Dried and painted plant materials are frequently used. With both modern and abstract designs, space is emphasised as part of the whole concept, but the finished designs should always contain the essential principles.

Other aspects of design
One very important element of design is the feeling of depth, and it is often missing from flower designs. In the jargon of the flower arranger, it is called recession. To achieve it, you simply cut some of the stems shorter than others, and push them deeper into the container. Recession gives any arrangement a degree of finesse and lends a professional touch.

It is always preferable to underplay rather than overfill an arrangement, for the space you leave around and within the design will heighten the beauty of the

MAKING A VERTICAL DESIGN

1 *Here a dish has been set into the top of a simple terracotta pot and filled with a block of wet oasis covered with wire netting. Alternatively you can fill the pot almost to the top with sand, then add the oasis and wire netting. This is particularly useful if the container is plastic or fairly light as it will be given greater stability.*

2 *Create the basic outline. It is important for a vertical design to soar upwards, so give it plenty of height.*

3 *Continue the arrangement by adding the flowers, still creating the upward flow of the design.*

4 *The completed arrangement. Vertical designs often have a very modern feeling, accentuated by the use of simple foliage. They are ideal for use in a confined space.*

flowers and foliage. A charming reminder of this is the saying often quoted by a friend of mine: 'Leave room for the butterflies!'.

As you work at an arrangement, it is very helpful to move away a little occasionally and survey your work with a critical eye. Check that any faults are not developing, as these are easier to spot from a short distance away. For example, flower heads should not be lying at the same level, or facing in the same direction. The mechanics must be covered too, and a feeling of naturalness, or flow, should be created.

There is really only one other important principle that I feel will help to create a good arrangement, and that is to arrange the design *in situ*. You may feel that that is easily done when working alone, but an entirely different matter when arranging flowers in front of strangers. However, once you've seen for yourself the benefits of this practice you will no doubt be converted to the idea, knowing that the success of your finished arrangement will easily outweigh any shyness or modesty you feel.

MAKING A PEDESTAL DESIGN

1 *Ensure that the mechanics for a pedestal are firm. Create the outline with seven stems.*

2 *The lowest stems are more easily placed in the arrangement underarm, and this also creates a more natural flow. Try placing the stem into the design both over and underarm and I am sure you will agree that the latter is a considerable improvement.*

3 *It is important to pay attention to the back of the pedestal, as it may well be visible. This photograph shows the back of the design and the way the mechanics have been hidden from view. Notice the stems flowing backwards, thus giving greater depth to the design.*

4 *The finished pedestal, after the addition of pink peonies, white ranunculus and green guelder roses.*

CHAPTER THREE

COLOUR

As yet I have not really mentioned colour, which is probably the only element of flower arranging that some people ever notice, as it is more important to them than texture and shape. Colour does give the greatest pleasure, and the endless combinations and contrasts can be very stimulating. In fact, colour is to the flower arranger what the palette is to the artist. Creating opportunities to stun or fascinate, to calm or thrill—such is the power of colour, and when used with imagination and style the results can be unforgettable.

Many people have wondered and marvelled at the varieties of colours in flowers and plants such as striped tulips, variegated ivies and ornamental kale, and all the panoply of brilliance that they display so wonderfully. In fact, it is a marvel that we can see colour at all.

What is colour?
Colour is the effect of light—nearly all of which comes from the sun—in a variety of wavelengths. These are mixed and so appear colourless. We can see the natural splitting of light to reveal the colours of a rainbow: the longest wavelength that we can see is red, and the shortest violet. We can only see the colours of plants because they are included in our range of vision.

Pigment, which is a substance found in parts of a plant cell, is responsible for colour. When light falls onto a pigment it absorbs and reflects different wavelengths. Pigments do not have a colour of their own but are often referred to as red, blue, and so on. For example, blue pigment looks blue because it absorbs all the other colours except blue, which it reflects.

Carotenoids are the red, yellow and orange pigments, which are much slower to break down than others. During leaf senescence (the time between maturity and leaf fall) their colours are temporarily revealed as all the glories of autumn. The carotenoids are also an essential substance for vision in animals, but as they are unable to produce this important substance for themselves they have to obtain it by eating plants or the animals that feed on those plants. Eating carrots to see in the dark is not the old wives' tale that many believe it

to be, and in fact plants provide us with the substance that enables us to see their beauty.

Beautiful as flowers are in themselves, it takes a little consideration to be able to display them to their best advantage. Some people have a flair for using colour and creating amazing arrangements, but not everyone is blessed with this ability, in which case they may need a few pointers before they can create special effects.

The relationship of colours
A colour wheel is a great help in choosing colour, because it clearly shows the ways in which flowers can work together or oppose each other. Look carefully at the outer band of the colour wheel (*see p. 30*), which shows the distinct colours called pure hues. These are red, orange, yellow, green, blue and violet. A tint is made by adding white to a pure hue, and a shade is created by adding black. To make a tone, you mix black and white together to make grey, then add it to a pure hue.

Colour schemes
Colour schemes using tints, tones and shades are described in several ways. Monochromatic colouring consists of tints, tones and shades of one colour. Analogous or adjacent colouring is the use of two or four colours that are closely related on the colour wheel. Complementary colouring uses colours that are directly or approximately opposite each other on the wheel. Triadic colouring uses three colours that are equidistant on the wheel, while polychromatic colouring is the use of many colours together.

Other dimensions are also helpful. Light value—or the amount of reflected colour—is called luminosity. Colours to which white has been added (tints are in this category) are more easily visible in dull or dim surroundings. Weight is yet another dimension, using tints and shades, that gives a sense of lightness or heaviness that is useful to the balance of the design.

The final group to be mentioned are the neutral, or achromatic, colours of black, white and grey. All other colours are chromatic. In reality, there are no plants or flowers that are completely true in colour,

This harmonious design (facing page) of lilies, lilac, guelder roses, sweet peas and eucalyptus has been created to please the eye. Its co-ordination, symmetry and compatibility with its surroundings give an extremely comfortable feeling.

and black tulips will always have a blue-black appearance while white flowers encompass a multitude of variations.

Creating atmosphere with colour

Colours also have the ability to create warmth, as in the case of reds and oranges, or coolness, as in the case of blues and greens. With this in mind you can use colour imaginatively to produce some very sensitive designs. In addition, colours can give a sense of movement: oranges and reds appear to come forward, blues recede,

yellows elevate and violets diminish. Green, however, remains neutral. The use of the illustration of movement in colour is fascinating, and well worth remembering when creating a design.

Background and harmony

Colour cannot be isolated from its surroundings, for the background will always have a profound effect on the colours you choose. Varying the backgrounds to a single design will aptly illustrate this point, and will show you

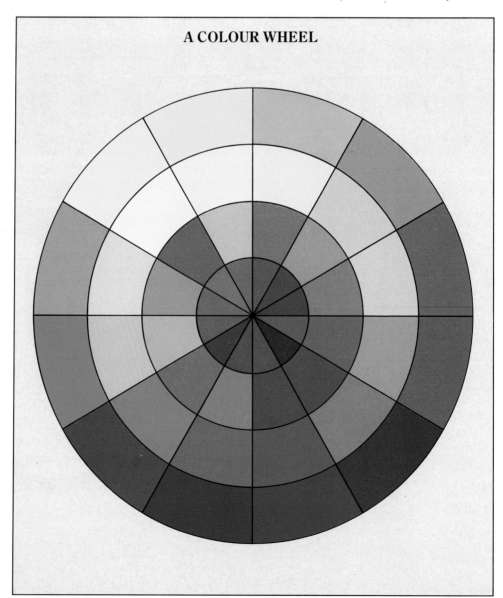

A COLOUR WHEEL

another reason why arranging flowers *in situ* is so very important.

Harmony is probably the most elusive quality to obtain in an arrangement, and is very much a matter of personal preference (as is most of flower arranging!) because no two people evaluate colour harmony in the same way. Quite simply, the effect must be pleasing to you—and hopefully to others who will view your arrangement as well.

While remembering, then, that the pleasure in harmony rests entirely in the eye of the beholder, here are one or two guidelines that may be of help. Firstly, using flowers and plants of equal colour weight will not always be effective, and graded colourings, such as deep coral through to apricot, can give a much more pleasing effect than when flowers of a single colour are used. Bright patches of colour should be used carefully, as dotting gaily-coloured flowers through an arrangement can create a very irritating effect. Colour grouping is usually better when you choose one dominant colour and then use variations of it. White flowers should be used with care, and arranging them in flowing lines will prevent them looking stark or strange. Good harmony shows co-ordination, symmetry and compatibility, as well as the sense of the arrangement being a complete whole.

Appreciating the colour around you
The more aware you are of colour, the greater your pleasure will be in visiting the countryside, parks and gardens. There is a new and wonderful world just waiting for you to discover—such as the magnificent colours of autumn, winter berries, leaves and fruits, shells on beaches, distant hills, mountains, dawns and sunsets. Once you are able to appreciate the extraordinary array of Nature's colours, the way you put flowers together is bound to improve immeasurably. You will also develop a new awareness by looking at the flowers themselves, and especially the delights of soft colourings. For instance, study the colours of hydrangeas as they fade, trusses of blackberries or the different greens in ornamental cabbages. The colours of fruits and plants will provide you with all the colour schemes you will ever need.

The pink tints and tones of the tulips, carnations, pinks and antirrhinums in this arrangement make it a monochromatic scheme.

CHAPTER FOUR

MECHANICS AND CONTAINERS

Just as the artist cannot work without brushes, paints and canvas, so too does the flower arranger need some tools of their particular trade. In this chapter, I shall describe the most essential pieces of equipment for the flower arranger.

Containers

These are, of course, of vital importance, since not only will they contain the arrangement, but in many cases they can also increase its effectiveness and attractiveness.

Unusual containers

It was Constance Spry who was the main inspiration behind the use of unusual containers, and these can be as varied as there are ideas. You need never worry that you don't have a suitable vase in which to arrange your flowers, because a little lateral

thinking should reveal the perfect container of one sort or another. For instance, any relatively well-stocked kitchen will yield a vast number of suitable containers: jugs, gravy and sauce boats, baking tins, vegetable dishes, and even the food and water bowls of animals can all be used with a little imagination.

Hunting in junk or thrift shops for unusual containers can be great fun, so don't imagine that all the best bargains have already been snapped up by enthusiastic flower arrangers, because they haven't! Old soup tureens or teapots, now without lids, are often inexpensive yet attractive, and you are unlikely to need the lid anyway! Don't be put off if an item, otherwise ideal, is cracked or damaged, because it may be easily repaired. Even if the piece you have chosen will not hold water it can be given a waterproof lining. Once you start looking,

Terracotta and pottery containers (right) *are ideal for all types of plant material, whether they are in the shape of formal tubs for planted trees or generously rounded jugs for flowers.*

Once you start looking around junk shops (facing page) *for interesting containers you will find an enormous variety from which to choose. The ideas are limitless and with a little ingenuity you should be able to convert all sorts of objects into containers for flowers.*

*China and silver
containers are amongst my
favourite choices for
flowers. They often lend
themselves to rather fragile
and delicate-looking
arrangements.*

you will see that the opportunities are
endless for finding interesting containers.
Happy hunting!

Vases
If you would prefer to buy a vase from a
shop, you may well be overwhelmed by the
array on offer. If so, try to avoid
succumbing to a sense of panic or confusion
that makes you buy the first thing you see in
the hope that it will do. Firstly, the colour
is important, and a neutral or earthy shade
is a very wise choice—it may be difficult

to find flowers that blend with very
strongly-coloured vases. As for shapes,
simple pottery urns and shallow oval or
round bowls are suitable for a variety of
floral designs. These shapes can also be
purchased in plastic (*see p. 38*). I like to
have pairs of identical containers or
pedestals whenever possible, as they
have so many more uses that way,
especially when one is creating
balanced arrangements on either side
of a mantelpiece, altar or doorway, for
example.

China containers

China, pottery and porcelain containers are all easily obtainable but are very fragile, and therefore may be the cause of much heartbreak if you have a habit of dropping things! Even so, you have a wide choice of shapes and designs, including pretty china baskets, shells supported by cherubs and sweetmeat dishes, and should be able to find the perfect containers to match your taste, style of arrangements, budget and home, whether they are found in antique or junk shops, or are good modern designs.

Metal containers

These are probably more practical than china and porcelain, and well-shaped bowls, jugs and mugs are readily available in copper, bronze, tin and brass. Some of these materials may also be given an antique appearance which means that they don't require cleaning! Silver is a lovely foil for flowers, and a great favourite of mine. In fact, an old silver chalice is probably my best-loved container and I always enjoy using it. An oval or rectangular silver entreé dish also looks very good on a dining table.

The warm colours of copper and brass make them especially suitable as flower containers, especially if you are able to make a feature of their wonderful reflections, smooth textures and lovely sheens.

Marble containers

Marble, alabaster and onyx are expensive stones, but they do make marvellous containers. Alabaster must be given an inner lining as water will roughen its surface. If the container is not a family heirloom, then a little clear varnish painted on the inside will prevent any water damage. The shapes and forms of these containers are beautiful and well worth the money spent, as their textures blend so well with the plant material.

Glass containers

Glass has recently been out of fashion, but there are some very good shapes to be found at the moment. I was recently reminded of the Munstead vases that were specially commissioned by Gertrude Jekyll. The simple designs are lovely, and when placing one within another, as she suggested, the possibilities are endless and exciting. What is more, her ideas can easily be adapted for modern glass containers. The only drawbacks with glass are that to look its best, it must be kept spotlessly clean, the flower water must always be clear and fresh, and the visible plant stems must look attractive.

Wooden containers

These are an interesting choice, and such containers as garden trugs, boxes, platters and bowls are ideal partners with plant material. Some of the most beautiful pedestals are wooden, making it a pleasure to use them, and very often they can take the place of a table in an arrangement.

Using baskets

Most arrangers own a basket, but it isn't always the most suitable shape. Invariably its handle is too short, and so is covered by the arrangement (unless it is very squat), thereby giving a most unsatisfactory design and effect. One of the best basket shapes to use is an old-fashioned picking basket, although you will have to line it first, with either tin or a sheet of black plastic.

Wall-mounted vases

Wall vases are not as popular as they once were, but nevertheless they are useful for a narrow hallway. Simple containers arranged on little shelves also look charming, and very elegant designs can be achieved with ivies and other downward-flowing plants.

Adapting unsightly containers

Many containers are made of plastic, but although some of them are available in very good shapes, their colours may leave much to be desired. Luckily, this can be easily remedied by repainting or spraying with aerosol paints. The real problem with plastic containers is their lightness, because although that makes them easy to transport from place to place, once they are filled with flowers they can become perilously top-heavy. Even if the plastic container feels heavy when first filled with wet oasis and water, once these dry out the container can easily topple over. To overcome this hazard you will have to weight the base, either with sand for a non-permanent weight or ready-mixed concrete for a permanent solution to the problem.

Plastic and fibreglass pillars are also extremely useful, although it is even more important that these should be adequately weighted to prevent accidents. They are generally white, and although this is agreeable, they are much more attractive when made to resemble such materials as stone, marble or terracotta (*see pp. 75–80*). Over the years I've had great fun transforming several pedestal shapes, and gained enormous use from them in the process.

Using bases

Very often an arrangement is given extra impact or height with the use of a base. These come in many guises, from beautifully designed metal, carved wood and Chinese-style designs, to simple wooden stands or even a cake board covered with the fabric of your choice. In many cases they give the design just the special touch that is required. On a practical note, the base can also protect the surface of furniture from water damage. (Accidents often happen, and leaves can happily syphon water over the edge of the container.) Protecting furniture is therefore essential, and an invaluable tip is to cover the underside of the base with a piece of plastic cut and trimmed to shape.

The cool, smooth contours of marble and alabaster are very beautiful, especially when enhanced by the particular beauty of fresh flowers and foliage.

Glass containers come in all shapes and sizes, and as well as the ones designed specially for the purpose, you can also put such objects as wine glasses, mustard pots and dessert bowls to good use in your arrangements.

Mechanics

Ensuring that your flowers stay in position in the container is your next consideration, and this is where the real tricks of the floristry trade are revealed! There are several methods from which to choose, and in time you will find that you use all of them for different occasions, and sometimes even all of them together!

Scissors

No arranger can work without scissors—not such an obvious statement as it may first appear! I know many arrangers who manage with old kitchen scissors or even a pair of dressmaking shears, not realising how much easier life would be with the proper kind. These are blunt-ended, with serrated blades and a small sharp inset curve that is specially designed to cut wires and stout branches. Light secateurs or a sharp knife can also be used.

Wire netting

Also known as chicken wire, wire netting is essential for successful flower arrangements, as it holds the flowers in position. Choose holes of either 3.75cm (1½in) or 5cm (2in). The cheapest is the best for this purpose, because it is also the finest mesh, and is available by the metre (yard) from any good ironmonger's.

Not so easy to find, and more costly, is a good-quality wire covered in soft plastic, but if you can track it down it is well worth the extra expense. For example, it doesn't scratch precious surfaces and, because the plastic is dark green in colour, it is less difficult to camouflage in an arrangement than the silver grey of galvanised wire.

To use the wire, first cut off the edging. Then take the container you plan to use and measure one-and-a-half times the diameter of the top by the width of the container plus approximately 7.5cm (3in). You will now realise how useful a pair of flower scissors can be! Roll the wire very loosely lengthways into a Swiss roll shape, then place in the container. The prongs at the sides should fit over the edge to keep the wire netting in place. Finally lift the centre of the netting a little. This roll of netting will give you several layers of wire and a variety of spaces into which you can place your

flowers. If your design is to be quite large and with heavy stems, then securing the netting with wire or string to the container, tying it as you would for a parcel, is a good idea. It can be cut away afterwards if not required.

Before arranging, you should check that the netting is secure. To do this, try to lift the container by the netting, but keep one hand under the container just in case! It should stay firm, and if it doesn't then you must start again. No flowers will stay in place if the mechanics are not stable. When working with glass containers, making a little netting cap that is placed over the top of the rim will hold the stems in place but be invisible once the plant material is in position. Oasis can be used in the top, but I always think it looks a little strange without the stalks showing!

Pin-holders

These are also useful devices for holding flowers in place, and are known as *kenzans* in the Japanese school of flower arranging. They are available in a wide variety of shapes and sizes.

A pin-holder has a heavy lead base, to give weight, in which sharp, pointed metal pins are embedded. When you buy a pin-holder do ensure that it has the required long sharp pointed pins, and don't be tempted to buy a cheaper version—it will soon become misshapen and useless. To prolong its life, keep it dry and clean when not in use.

Often the pin-holder will need to be held in place very firmly, especially when you plan to use heavy branches and the like. To do this, press a thin circle or small lumps of Plasticine or adhesive clay on the bottom of the pin-holder, then press it firmly into the container. Even greater support can be given by pressing a little crumpled wire netting into the pins.

Oasis

Oasis is a water-retaining plastic foam that you will either love or hate, but it does have its advantages. Rather like a sponge, oasis absorbs water, but it remains firm enough to allow stems and branches to be pushed into it, and then holds them in place while supplying them with moisture. Not all plants

When using a wooden container try to let the beauty of the wood enhance your arrangement. In most cases you will have to protect the wood from water by using a waterproof lining or placing a smaller container of water inside the wooden one.

like oasis, but many do, taking up as much water as they need and revelling in the moist humid atmosphere that the foam creates.

Although not all flower arrangers like oasis, one of its benefits is that it allows you to create flower designs that would not be possible with wire netting and pin-holders alone, and it is very useful for creating a downward flow of plant material. It also prevents the plant stems from rotting.

Ideally, once an arrangement is finished you should store the damp oasis in a plastic bag to keep it moist, but even if the oasis has dried out completely you can revitalise it by adding a small amount of washing-up liquid to the water that you will use for re-soaking. If the foam has been used several times and now seems to have served its purpose, it can be placed in a plastic bag with a little water and a drop of washing-up liquid, and crushed. You can then press it into the awkward corners of unusually-shaped containers that would be difficult to fill with solid oasis. Surprisingly, washing-up liquid does not affect oasis at all, but it will have to be thrown away if left in stale flower water. Turning the oasis upside down can also give it a new lease of life.

There are several types of oasis on the market, intended for differing uses such as soft spring stems, so do check that you are buying the right kind for the flowers you will be using. Oasis is cheapest when bought in large bricks, which you can then cut up according to your needs and soak well in cold water for the amount of time specified by the manufacturers before using. Buckets or a zinc bath are ideal for soaking oasis, although I have a wire basket set in my sink which is not only marvellous for the dishes but also very useful for lifting the wet blocks of oasis out of the water to allow them to drain!

Several good accessories are available to hold the oasis firmly in a container. One is a heavy lead base with widely-spaced pins that looks rather like a near-bald pin-holder, but is very useful and can be secured to a container with adhesive clay or Plasticine for greater stability. A similar, but smaller, device is known as a frog, and is often sold with an adhesive base. It is ideal for smaller arrangements.

Baskets and wickerwork look especially attractive when combined with plant material, and there is a wide range of styles, shapes and textures from which to choose. The container will have to be given a waterproof lining before it is used.

42

USING WIRE NETTING

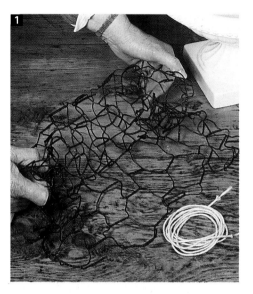

1 *Always try to use plastic-covered wire netting when working with china vases as it protects their surface. Roll the netting into a Swiss roll shape and then place in the vase, lifting the centre a little and making sure the wire is well spaced.*

2 *Hold the netting in place with string, tying it as you would a parcel and catching the string into the netting occasionally. If the netting is not secure the flowers will move about in the container and render the mechanics useless. Once the netting is firm, fill the vase with fresh water.*

Florists' tubes and cones
Made of metal or plastic, tubes and cones are a great asset and are invaluable when you need to give added height to the flowers or foliage in an arrangement. They are either pushed into the wire or oasis or securely attached to a cane or green garden stick to give even greater height. The cones or tubes themselves should be filled with wire or oasis in which the material can be arranged.

Candlecups
Very useful yet inexpensive, candlecups are made from metal or plastic and are used to make arrangements with candlesticks. The candlecup is placed into the space left for the candle, but oasis usually has to be placed in the surround. This mechanic is very effective and allows one to create a good downward design using very little plant material. Once the arrangement is completed, the candle is replaced in its recess.

Aprons
If you do a lot of flower arranging, an apron with pockets is extremely useful, especially if it slips on over your head and ties at the back. An apron pocket is the ideal place in which to tuck your scissors, reel wire and other small mechanics when you are in the middle of creating an arrangement, because scissors especially can disappear among foliage, even if they have red or orange handles. Much valuable time can be saved if you keep them handy in your apron pocket!

The simple waist apron can become uncomfortable after a while as it has to be fastened fairly tightly to stay in place—and if you've put a heavy pair of scissors and a reel of wire in one of the pockets slipping can certainly be a problem! A plastic apron with pockets is a good idea, but can become rather warm in hot weather. A simple linen or cotton apron may well be the best choice, because not only will it be more comfortable to wear but it will also be easy to wash.

Work boxes
Another helpful idea, particularly if you are working away from home, is a box or container in which to keep all your

These are a few of the essential accessories needed to arrange flowers effectively – pin-holders, reel wires, tapes, florists' scissors and oasis.

A little cap of netting is all that is needed when preparing the mechanics for a small glass vase. Stretch the netting over the mouth of the vase, hooking the prongs over the rim to hold it in place. Once again, plastic-covered netting is best.

USING OASIS

1 When using oasis in the vase, fix an oasis holder firmly in the bottom of the vase with adhesive clay or Plasticine.

2 Put the wet oasis on top of the oasis holder then tape it in place, pressing it firmly on to the sides of the vase. White tape is more easily hidden on a white vase than green tape.

mechanics and equipment. The divided work boxes that are made from plastic and are used by carpenters and the like are marvellous, and very cheap to buy. The divisions are very handy and will take all your equipment, including florists' tape, wire, string, knives, scissors, adhesives, pins, glue and so on. Extras such as wedges and additional bases will fit happily in the bottom of the box.

Brushes and brooms
If creating an arrangement away from home, you will not be required to clean before you start work (although I have had to do this on occasion), but you will have to clear and clean up after you have finished working. This is part of the job, whether you like it or not, and no one will be very pleased if you leave a mess behind you, so do be prepared to clear away afterwards.

Through experience, I have learned to always make it plain that I will clear away my own arrangements when they are no longer needed. This enables me to remove any mechanics that I wish to keep, as well as any treasured containers that I've used. Otherwise, some well-intentioned helper may not realise how expensive pin-holders are to replace, nor how much you value that chipped soup tureen, and throw them away with the rest of the rubbish! If you won't be able to clear away the faded arrangement, then you may prefer to use simple plastic trays and the cheapest mechanics. This won't mean that you skimp on the arrangement—simply that you won't be so out of pocket if the worst happens and they are accidentally discarded.

A dustpan and brush is a great help, as is a soft broom if you are working in a church or hall. A mopping-up cloth is an absolute essential, since even the best arrangers have accidents, and you must always be prepared for them. A plastic bag into which you can place the wet cloth is also useful, and a duster is necessary if you need to polish a shiny surface or clear away any small pieces of flowers or foliage.

Buckets and watering cans
Ideally, you should have three buckets for conditioning, and although you can get by with the ordinary household type, the best

bucket for the flower arranger is specially made of plastic with solid handles on either side, making it much easier to pick up when loaded with flowers and water. The normal handle invariably decapitates the bucket's contents! Florists' flower buckets are available in two sizes, although very small flowers can be conditioned in any container that will hold enough water and provide adequate support. A child's beach bucket or even aspirin bottles are very good!

A watering can with a long spout is invaluable, and a fine mister spray for freshening up plant material is also very useful. A dust sheet or plastic cover is essential, because not only can it be used to carry your plant material but it also protects floors and furniture, and can be used when removing the rubbish afterwards. Try to find one that has integral handles, which will make it easier to carry. You can also buy an excellent large plastic bag which is fitted into a simple lightweight frame on wheels, making an instant wheelbarrow—a wonderful way to lighten the load you sometimes have to carry.

First aid kits
Sharp knives and scissors can cause accidents, so always carry a mini first aid kit around with you. Pack it with plasters and an antiseptic cream and also include an ointment that will ease insect bites—often a hazard when working with flowers.

Another important part of your equipment, if you will be working away from home, is a flask of hot coffee or tea, or perhaps some cold drinks in the summer. It is always a good idea to have a short rest in the midst of arranging flowers, as not only will it give you a breather but you will also have the chance to contemplate your designs from a distance, and correct any glaring faults or mistakes that may become apparent.

As you may have appreciated by now, good mechanics are an essential element of successful flower arranging, but the golden rule to remember is that they must not be visible in the finished design. So, whenever you create an arrangement, be it tiny or enormous, make sure that you practise the art of invisible mechanics!

CHAPTER FIVE

USING SILK FLOWERS

Silk flower arrangements are a marvellous decorative idea for the home, and although they can be used on their own, they can be particularly effective when incorporated with fresh foliage. It is best to choose long-lasting types of foliage, such as laurel, fatsia and elaeagnus, and you should also select interesting shapes and colours, and contrasting textures.

Silk flowers have improved in quality tremendously over the past few years and there is now a vast number from which to choose, but it is always well worth taking a little time and trouble when you buy them. Colouring is especially important, and some silk flowers can look very garish and gaudy. Softer and more neutral shades are easier to live with and will be much more versatile. Remember, you will probably own them for a long time!

Creating an arrangement with silk flowers

It is best to make a few adjustments to the silk flowers before putting them in an arrangement, because they can look very stiff, especially when viewed with fresh foliage. Giving each stem a slight twist will soften its shape, thereby creating a more natural feel. If there are several flower heads on one stem, it is a good idea to remove a couple, then rewire and tape them into a different shape, as flowers are not naturally identical. If there are any buds, it is particularly lifelike if these are rewired on longer stems.

Now arrange your design as you would if you were using fresh flowers, paying attention to the height, depth and focal point. Don't be tempted to shorten the wire stems by turning them back on themselves, but cut them as though they were fresh. They can easily be rewired at a later date if you then need longer stems. I have seen some silk flowers with very mangled and bent stems that consequently demolish any oasis into which they are pushed and ruin the shape of wire netting.

It is important to keep the container charged with water as, although the silk flowers will happily survive without water, the foliage won't. Wiping the foliage occasionally with a proprietary brand of leaf shine will keep it looking its best—dusty foliage does little to recommend any arrangement. You can also dust the silk flowers carefully *in situ*, or remove them from the arrangement and give them a gentle blow with warm air from a hair dryer.

Seasonal arrangements

Making arrangements with a combination of silk and fresh flowers or foliage is particularly useful at those times of the year when fresh plant material is very scarce or expensive. However, if you want the arrangement to look authentic you must choose silk flowers appropriate to the season! For that reason, you may find it useful to invest in such silk flowers as roses, carnations and others that are available all year round, rather than choose any that are authentic for only a couple of weeks every year.

Christmas decorations containing a mixture of silk flowers and fresh foliage can be very attractive and festive, especially if you use hollies or ivies with silk carnations or poinsettias. Using silk flowers, such as chrysanthemums in muted colours, with dried and glycerined material (*see p. 58*) is another lovely idea for winter arrangements, and driftwood is also effective when used with silk flowers.

The foliage in this pedestal design is so attractive that it could easily stand on its own, without further embellishment. See over the page for two designs where artificial flowers have been added.

47

The addition of these artificial lilies brings out different shades in the foliages and lends a very different atmosphere to the arrangement.

Here, some large apricot-coloured silk peonies have been added to the design. They are particularly suitable for arrangements in places of worship, but look equally attractive in other, more secular, settings.

49

CHAPTER SIX

DECORATIVE IDEAS

By now, the basic flower designs and shapes should be familiar to you, and you may well be enjoying a greater sense and understanding of colour than ever before, just by opening your eyes to your surroundings and studying the intricate and subtle colourings of plants. The next step is to make flower arrangements that are rather more unusual and exciting and, because ideas for these are never-ending, I will be showing you just a few examples which I hope will act as a useful and inspiring springboard and encourage you to start experimenting with decorative schemes of your own.

Table decorations
Often hurriedly arranged at the last minute before guests arrive for lunch or dinner, table decorations can suffer from being rather dull and boring. This is made worse by the fact that they will be on show for the duration of the meal and can therefore be minutely observed by the entire party!

Since it is perfectly feasible to arrange flowers at least the day before the event—if not two—you should therefore have plenty of time in which to create a masterpiece, or at least a talking point!

Making successful table decorations
When planning a table decoration, remember the florist's golden rule of making the arrangement suitable to its setting. Perhaps the most important point to remember is that all the guests must be able to see each other—it will be extremely tiring, not to say irritating, for them to have to peer around masses of foliage and flowers whenever they wish to talk to each other! You must also leave enough room on the table for the plates, glasses, dishes, condiments and so on, and if you will be using candles they should be part of the scheme and not look like an afterthought. One can buy candles in marvellous colours, but do make sure that they blend in with the colour scheme of the arrangement. Ivory-coloured candles are always a good stand-by and usually look pleasing with most flowers, even white ones.

The flowers and foliage will be under close scrutiny, so try to use perfect materials whenever possible. Avoid any

MAKING A SIDE TABLE ARRANGEMENT

1 *Assemble the mechanics to give a tall narrow design of foliage and flowers, and allowing space at the base of the design for the fruit which will give a sense of solidity. Into a baking tin I placed a block of oasis covered with wire netting, on top of which I placed a large florists' tube filled with netted oasis. This was all placed on a large piece of wood.*

2 *Arrange the outline, placing the heaviest fruit first. Hold the fruit in place with barbecue sticks, the lighter berries with wooden cocktail sticks and wire the cherries.*

3 *Once you are happy with the arrangement of the fruits, add the flowers. Here I used a profusion of brightly-coloured poppies, allowing them to fall into their own curves naturally.*

50

MAKING A CANDLESTICK ARRANGEMENT

1 *Place a special mould on the candlestick, and fit a candle into its holder with the follower and shade. Cut a piece of oasis to the correct shape, soak it and then press it into the mould. Create the outline with foliage and downward-flowing plant material.*

2 *Add the flowers to the design. Simplicity is the key to elegance, and here the summer jasmine and 'Champagne' roses combine well to give a soft effect.*

3 *The followers give an added dimension to the candlesticks, and the candlelight shining on to the flowers and foliage helps to create an intimate atmosphere that is ideal for a formal dinner party.*

MAKING A
BUFFET TABLE
ARRANGEMENT

1 *Place two large pieces of oasis into the base of each urn and cover with wire netting. Here, the urn has been put on a marble base that is really a wooden box painted to resemble marble (see p. 77).*

2 *Create the outline with fine plant material. It is very important to arrange this design* in situ, *because it would be extremely difficult to move it around once it were finished. The damask tablecloth has therefore been protected to prevent it being stained or splashed.*

3 *Complete the design by adding the flowers and some soft flowing plant material. This enhances the effect of the lilies and carnations and makes the design look more interesting.*

4 *The completed buffet table arrangement, with matching urns. The flower garland and swags of ribbon (see pp. 65–7) have been added to increase the decorative and festive appearance of the table.*

nibbled or torn leaves or damaged flowers, and, of course, ensure that none of the mechanics show.

White porcelain containers look wonderful when placed on white lace cloths, silver entreé dishes look good on polished wood, and wooden bowls are effective on pine tables, although as you begin to experiment you will find your own favourites. Placing the container on a base will help to give a downward flow to the arrangement and can also improve the design. If using candlesticks, these should be in keeping with the container both in colour and texture.

Candlestick arrangements
Using a candlestick as a container is a very practical move: it confines the arrangement to a limited area and turns the candle and flowers into a single unit. One charming idea is to incorporate a candle follower and shade with the candle. A candle follower is a metal frame that fits over the candle (it must be the Georgian straight-sided kind), and then carries the shade which is made from metal or stiff card. Once assembled, it creates a very attractive and intimate feeling.

Candlestick arrangements nearly always benefit from the inclusion of downward-flowing flowers and foliage, unless they are very short, in which case a simple garland looks charming. Always keep your flowers clear of the candles, as they can constitute a considerable fire hazard, and always replace the candles when they begin to burn down near the flowers—no matter how exciting you want the occasion to be, watching the flower arrangements going up in flames is too dramatic for most people's taste!

Side table arrangements
An arrangement on a sideboard or side table is a good opportunity to let your imagination run riot, and the use of fruits and berries is especially effective. In most cases, the height of the arrangement is unlimited and, unless the surface will be needed for serving or storing the china or wine, then this will also be yours to command. It is best to link the colour scheme for this arrangement with that of the table, but it

MAKING AN ARRANGEMENT FOR A HALL

1 *First prepare the driftwood and mechanics by screwing them on to a base, setting them into cement or clamping them in place. Here, they have been pressed firmly on to a special pin-holder. Whichever method is chosen, it is important that the driftwood should be secure.*

2 *Create the outline with some well-defined foliage. Here, variegated elaeagnus has been used. Its leaves respond very well to being sponged with water, and perhaps wiped with a proprietary leaf shine, which reveals their marvellous colourings.*

3 *Add a few scarlet parrot tulips to create a natural yet striking design that allows the driftwood to be seen to its best advantage.*

isn't essential, particularly if fruit is being used. When creating this type of design it is often better to forgo a traditional container and use two bases and a simple tin, such as a bread bin, for the mechanics. It will not be seen in the finished design, yet will make life much easier for you when arranging such fruits as pineapples and grapes. Potted plants, for example *Begonia rex* or caladiums, can also be set into the design more easily. Trailing ivy, whether cut or left in pots, is very effective when used to soften the arrangement and blend all the fruits together.

Buffet tables
A buffet table is always a pleasure to decorate, and there are several lovely ideas that can be used. However, you should check a couple of essential points before finalising your plans: will the table be centrally placed or to the side?; will guests help themselves or be served with food? If professional caterers are being used, don't hesitate to ask their advice. They will appreciate your concern and will be able to suggest the best positions from their standpoint. Be prepared to compromise a little in order to obtain the best results for everyone concerned.

Arrangements placed at each end of the table are generally a satisfactory idea, and they can be as important or as tall as the occasion and setting demands. If you want to create a greater impact then garlands and swags draped around the sides of the table or cloth are enchanting. They can be easily made from *Myrsiphyllum asparagoides*, better known as smilax—long lengths of very attractive green foliage that lasts well out of water. Smilax always looks graceful looped up with ribbon bows or posies. Using flower garlands in the same way can look exquisite, but these are very time-consuming to make. Ivies, clematis and similar trailing plants can be used, and old man's beard, *Clematis vitalba*, looks wonderful if it has first been allowed to stand in a solution of glycerine and water until the leaves change colour (this process takes anything up to six weeks). It develops a beautiful colouring of brown and cream and when combined with autumnal berries and flowers can be quite stunning.

MAKING A VEGETABLE CONE

1 *This design is worked on a large brass tray with an inner smaller dish that holds the mechanics. Place a cone securely in the oasis and wire it firmly, then place a narrower cone behind it to give even greater height. Push barbecue sticks into the vegetables and arrange the heaviest at the base. The tomatoes are wired and taped in string.*

2 *Fill in the design, taking care to maintain its conical shape. Peas and French beans look good wired into groups. You can cut radishes into flower shapes to add interest. Carefully make incisions across each radish in three directions, place in a bowl of water and leave in the refrigerator for a few hours until they have opened up to resemble flowers. Push wooden cocktail sticks into them before arranging.*

3 *Finish the arrangement, taking care not to overfill the design and covering any remaining visible mechanics with heads of parsley. You can add daisies, daisy chrysanthemums or cobs of corn to make an attractive Harvest supper arrangement. For an informal party in a kitchen you could make matching arrangements to sit at either end of the table.*

Decorating with driftwood

You can make very good designs from driftwood, which is a treasure that I believe every flower arranger should possess. Invariably one hears tales of finding exciting and beautiful driftwood on the beach or on holiday, but I have never been that lucky (although I keep looking!). Instead, I've always had to buy mine! Driftwood is the description of wood that has been aged in one of several ways: cleaned and scoured by the sea; burnt and bleached by fire; or old pieces that have rotted and been reshaped by the weather and animals. To

me, it is as beautiful as a piece of sculpture.

If you are in woodland and do see an interesting piece of wood, there are several dos and don'ts to remember if you want to collect it. Firstly, do check that you are entitled to take it away! If you are, then wrap it in paper and put it into a plastic bag for the journey home. (Anything could crawl out of it!) Secondly, don't leave your driftwood in the house until you have cleaned it thoroughly, for the same reason. You can do this by soaking it in water for several days. Some people use bleach, but it changes the colour, so I prefer to use

WORKING WITH STATUARY

1 *When arranging flowers or foliage with any sort of statuary it is very important to work in* situ, *otherwise the design will not feel complete. Here the outline is being created around the figure and stand which have been painted to look like stone. I have used florists' tubes to increase the height of the arrangement.*

2 *Now build up the design using the heavier plant material. At this stage it doesn't matter if any mechanics are still visible.*

3 *Complete the arrangements by adding the rest of the flowers and making sure you have hidden all the mechanics. Here, two arrangements have been used to frame the entrance to a garden marquee.*

plain water. Then I give the wood a good scrub to remove any remaining dirt or inhabitants, before allowing it to dry completely.

I prefer to leave driftwood in its natural state, but it can be polished or coloured with wood dyes. The danger with this, of course, is that you may not like the finished result, and want to burn it or give it to a flower arranging friend who does like it. If you do the latter, then be prepared to see them use it in a marvellous way that will make you furious with yourself at having parted with it!

If you will be keeping your piece of driftwood, take a good look at it from every angle. Once you have found a position you like, set it down onto a base—a simple piece of wood is ideal. Set a flat dish, containing your mechanics, either behind or within the wood, but remember that it always looks most attractive with the minimum of materials, and just looks messy if smothered with flowers and foliage. Nevertheless, a great variety of materials can be used, although driftwood is particularly useful when plant materials are scarce. For example, frosted driftwood with holly and robins makes a delightful Christmas decoration, and a few daffodils or a potted primrose is a charming spring arrangement. Flowering shrubs are natural companions, and camellias and their foliage are a real joy. Decorations in halls and entrances are always a pleasure, and are especially attractive when driftwood is incorporated in them.

Decorating with vegetables
I have already suggested using fruits and berries, but vegetables can make marvellous designs too. Arranging with vegetables is not a new idea, but it is great fun, especially if you present them in imaginative ways. You can use variegated kale, as though it were a flower, to make a dramatic centre piece, gently push the husks of sweetcorn back to reveal the corn beneath, or split celery or fennel in half to show their insides. Aubergines, peppers and courgettes, to name a few, have magnificent depths of colour and lovely sheens, and artichokes, cauliflowers, carrots, onions and sprays of peas or beans

are just some of the vegetables that make fascinating shapes in arrangements.

Unless you are going to perform a tricky balancing act with the vegetables, you will need to use sticks and wires to hold them in place, and may well find it easiest to build up your arrangement around a conical base. You can then cover any visible mechanics with parsley, moss or something similar.

Designs incorporating statuary
Using a figurine, bust or statue in an arrangement can look extremely elegant, but you will have to plan the design carefully first. The difficulty is to make the arrangement look like a harmonious whole, rather than a floral design that just happens to be sitting next to a piece of statuary, or a complete jungle of plant material through which the figure can barely be glimpsed!

Choose a base that will unite the piece of statuary and the plant material, then find a simple tin for the mechanics and flowers which can be placed close to the figure. I have not yet mentioned drapes (lengths of materials which are allowed to fall into natural folds behind or within the design), and indeed I very rarely use them, but fabric, figures and flowers seem to combine very well. Again, the drapes must enhance the arrangement and not look like an accidental placing, so your choice of material is very important. A soft neutral colour is useful, and silk is a particularly good choice of fabric, as it falls into marvellously elegant folds (though sometimes it needs a little help!). You can create a very smart effect if the drape and base are made from the same material.

When working with a piece of statuary, it is particularly important for the design to be created *in situ*, with the figure, base, fabric and container set up ready for the flowers and foliage. Line designs always work well with figurines.

Busts or statues are a marvellous excuse to create a spectacle, especially if they are loosely decorated with soft garden flowers and foliage that appear to be growing through, over, in and around them. Garlands are also enchanting. These ideas can look particularly stunning at parties given in gardens or conservatories or wedding receptions held in marquees.

CHAPTER SEVEN

GARLANDS, SWAGS, PLAQUES AND CONES

I adore garlands, and find them one of the most attractive decorative ideas of all. Whether they are made from flowers, flowers and foliage or just foliage, they can be used in all sorts of exciting and attractive ways and, although they do take a long time to make, the finished results are well worth the effort. The way in which a garland is made will depend on the situation for which it is intended.

Making garlands with wire and moss
Fresh flowers really cannot be bettered for garlands, so try to use them whenever possible. To make a garland with fresh flowers, cut a piece of 5-cm (2-in) wire netting 20–22cm (8–9in) long (the green plastic-covered variety is preferable). Place the wire flat on a table, then arrange sphagnum moss along its length as though filling a cigarette paper. The moss is readily available and usually sold in plastic bags—make sure it is moist. Fold the wire over and hook its prongs together to seal the join. Then press down gently on the joined side, leaving one rounded and one flat side. This will make a garland about 7.5cm (3in) thick. Large garlands should be about 12.5cm (5in) thick, and very delicate ones about 2.5cm (1in) thick.

Choose fairly small plant material, such as box foliage or pittosporum, and push it into the frame and moss first, followed by the flowers. If you need longer garlands they can be made in sections and then wired together. It looks very elegant if the centre of the garland is the focal point, with all the leaves facing in that direction. If the garland will look better when tapered at both ends, then squeeze the wire netting a little tighter. A drop for the garland can be made in the same way, but you must taper the end carefully and use the flowers and foliage more sparingly. This method has the advantage of giving the garland an attractive, ready-made, background to the moss, which has a decorative appearance.

Making garlands with oasis
An alternative is to make garlands with bricks of wet oasis that have been cut into four or eight lengthwise, according to the thickness of garland required. These are either wrapped in fine polythene and joined with sticky tape, or pushed into a stitched tube of polythene. Making lengths of eight or so 'sausages' is best, and you should allow a length of polythene at either end to enable them to be joined together. If a long length is needed, they are tied together with string. Do not cut the string between each block, but take it along each length as this will stop the garland sagging when the flowers and foliage are in place. Once you have made the garland to the required length, it is quite simple to push the foliage and flowers into the oasis through the polythene, and the finer this is the easier it can be pierced by the plant stems. If you have any problems, you can make a hole first with a darning needle or wooden toothpick.

All the small pretty flowers look delightful in these garlands, including pinks, all-year-round chrysanthemums, roses and berries. You can also make garlands out of rope, binding the flowers and foliage on to it, but it does tend to twist and is not so effective.

Making garlands of dried flowers
Either the moss or oasis bases can be used for garlands of dried flowers and glycerined foliage, but I prefer to wire the plant material together piece by piece. Although it takes a considerable time, it produces a much more delicate and elegant design. Dried gypsophila and roses and their leaves all look wonderful when used in this way. Each component is wired individually, then they are gradually wired in with gutta percha or stem tape in a suitably toning shade.

Making plaques
These are made in a similar fashion but need a base on which to rest. It should be slightly smaller than the finished plaque, with the materials wired on individually to build up the design and hopefully to create the effect of Grinling Gibbons' work. These designs often look better if created or painted in tones that match the walls or pillars on which they will be placed, and I find it easier to work from the narrowest end first.

Making linen bows
The wonderful ribbons and bows that were carved and painted so beautifully by such

MAKING A WIRED GARLAND

1 *Cut a strip of wire netting that will be as long as the garland you wish to make. Then cut away the edging to the wire netting and place the moss along the centre of the netting.*

2 *Pull the netting up around the moss and hook the prongs around each other to secure the netting properly. Press down gently on one side to make it a little flatter than the other.*

3 *Decorate the garland with wired foliage and flowers. This is quite economical because the moss helps to make an attractive background.*

craftsmen as Grinling Gibbons and Ehret are a delight, especially with their pretty shapes, tucks and folds, and it is very pleasing to incorporate such ideas in garlands, swags and plaques—they can even be part of the design itself. Unfortunately you cannot achieve the right folds with soft ribbon, or even flower ribbon, although it is quite stiff. You can use wired ribbon, but it isn't always easy to find. Tarlatan is an inexpensive muslin that can be starched into shape, but it quickly becomes damp and limp, spoiling the effect completely! I think that linen bows are the answer, and although rather time-consuming to make, they are well worth the effort and really do seem to last forever. I made some about ten years ago and they're still going strong, having been repainted and re-used many times.

Suitable fabrics
Choose the fabric you will be using before actually beginning work. Cotton is best, but avoid nylon or silky materials as they are not suitable. You do not have to buy the cotton specially—old teacloths, tablecloths or sheeting are ideal, and if you don't have anything suitable to hand, a hunt around a thrift or junk shop should soon provide you with plenty of inexpensive fabrics. I generally use a rough teacloth for a kitchen garland, and ribbon or fine sheeting for the drapes on a swag. Old torn handkerchiefs are ideal for making small delicate bows.

Stiffening the fabric
Firstly, you must stiffen the fabric, using one of two methods—either a flour and water paste or a proprietary brand of papier mâché. Both are equally efficient, but I would only recommend the former if you can keep the finished result away from mice and other animals—I have lost several bows and decorations to hungry rodents who must find it a delicious pastry! You can buy ready-to-mix packs of papier mâché from good art shops, but store it carefully in a dry place if you won't be using it immediately as it could easily become mildewed otherwise.

Place the flour or papier mâché powder in a bowl, then pour in some cold water and mix well with a spoon. Only add a little cold

Here, a wired garland of flowers and foliage has been looped around a piece of garden statuary – a decoration that would be ideal for an outdoor party or wedding reception.

MAKING A FOAM GARLAND

1 *Cut wet oasis into fairly small lengths and place them along lengths of fine polythene sheeting before joining the sides together with sticky tape. Then take string along the length, tying each 'sausage' along the row to prevent it stretching. Then insert flowers and foliage through the plastic into the foam, first using a darning needle to pierce the plastic if necessary.*

2 *Here the finished garland has been used to decorate a box topiary tree. The garland is held in position with stub wires bent into the shape of hair pins.*

You can also make garlands from dried flowers and foliage. To do this, wire each piece of plant material then tape all the pieces together to form a very delicate and long-lasting design. You can use a variety of interesting materials, including berries and nuts.

water at a time, and stir well until the mixture has the consistency of whipped cream.

Tear or cut your chosen fabric into strips that are twice the width of the finished ribbons. Naturally the length is for you to decide, but unless you are going to make a vast design, a metre (yard) is usually adequate. Cover the working table with a sheet of thick plastic, then place the strips of fabric on top of it. (The plastic is only to contain the messy mixture and can be dispensed with if your work surface is easily cleaned, although you may find it easiest to lift up the whole plastic sheet when moving the fabric prior to drying it.)

Although you can work with bare hands, you may find it more pleasant to use thin disposable plastic gloves. Take a little of the mixture and smear it all over the first strip, then fold the outside edges into the centre, press down and smooth the mixture all through the fabric. Smear more mixture over the strip and ensure that it is completely covered. There is no need to swamp the fabric in a thick layer of paste, as a light cover is all that is required. Repeat the process on the other pieces. These do not have to be exactly alike or even entirely covered with the mixture.

Making the bow shapes
While the fabric is still wet, tie the pieces into the bow, or any other shape that is required. You will be able to use a single strip to make a small bow but must make

two halves and join them together for larger ones. This is a little sticky and may take several attempts before you get the right shape, so don't give up! Then leave to dry—depending on the thickness of the bows and ribbons, this can take between one and three days. You can leave them for longer, as it is important that the bows are allowed to dry out completely. If you are still unhappy with the shape while a bow is drying, you can damp it down and remould it. You may even wish to add more mixture to give a smoother finish, or perhaps to create deeper creases. I usually remould and fiddle with the bows for quite a while before I'm happy with them.

Painting the bows
Before you begin to paint the bows, you must check that they are bone dry. If not, they will soften and sag quickly once the paint is applied, and it will take longer than usual to dry out. Of course, the colour in which you paint the bows will be determined by the design for which they are intended, and you could gild them for Christmas, paint them pale blue for a wedding or silver for a party, and so on, according to your needs. However, the basic colours I use are very dark brown, grey, black or very dark green.

Cover the bows with a coat of matt emulsion paint and leave to dry. You can use a matt aerosol spray if you wish. Once this is dry, mix up some emulsion paint until it is a muddy grey-green and partially paint the bows with it, gently pulling the brush over the base coat. Allow to dry. Finally, you can add the colour of your choice, allowing some of the duller colour and the grey-green to show, particularly in the folds. Soft grey-green is more acceptable if the bows are to be pale blue, pink, lemon, white and so on. Don't omit the dark undercoat because it will give depth—just painting the ribbons in one colour will create a very flat feeling. Once the bows are completely dry, thread wire through their backs and use them as you wish.

Using the bows
The Grinling Gibbons designs are always improved with the addition of painted ribbon bows draped or tied into the designs. I usually make mine so that they resemble stone as I find wood very hard to simulate, although one day I hope to crack the problem! The designs look very elegant when set against stone walls and pillars, and sometimes I decorate them with a little light foliage.

Painting plastic or dried fruits and vegetables to make them look old can also give very pleasing results, whether they are used for plaques, topiary, cones or wreaths. In fact, the possibilities are endless, especially if you can set off your designs with the painted linen bows to create a pottery or sculptured feeling.

Making cones
Plaques and wall hangings are great fun, and the more unusual the shape, the more exciting the end result. Cones are particularly useful, at all times of the year, and they can be made from fresh or dried material and used with ribbons, as the Byzantines did. They can be as large or as small as you wish, and the way in which they are made is similar although the amount of plant material will vary.

As with the garlands, your finished design will be larger than the initial frame, so remember to adjust your mechanics accordingly. Cut a piece of wire netting into the shape of a triangle, then join the sides together to form a cone and pack tightly with sphagnum moss, then cover with greenery before decorating in whichever way you wish. Alternatively, you can fill the frame with wet oasis. If the cone is to be very large, you can fill the centre of the frame with newspaper. Flowers, fruits and berries can then be used for the decoration, but you must take care not to lose the overall shape which is classical, and should be kept as such. You will have great fun working on cones, and it takes surprisingly little material to create a stunning design.

Cones look very good placed on simple bases, be they cake stands or elegant columns, and they make attractive designs that are suitable for all sorts of occasions. You can easily make them in advance, because they will keep perfectly for a week or two if well sprayed with water. You can always add special flowers when the cones are finally needed.

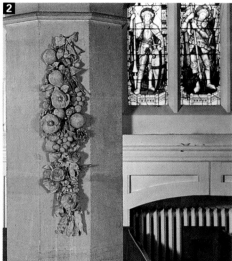

MAKING A PLAQUE

1 *A plaque is made in a
similar way to a dried
garland* (see pp. 66–7), *in
that all the materials must
be wired together, but they
are then wired on to a solid
wooden base, to give a
firmer design.*

2 *This finished plaque
has been mounted on a
church pillar, and painted
to match its stonework to
give the feeling of an
integral design. Often the
plaque is worked centrally
on a base that is larger
than the design.*

*This round wall design
has been worked in the
same way as the stone-
coloured plaque, but
painted gold. The design
incorporates some
intertwining ribbons that
were especially made for
the purpose* (see pp. 63–
70).

MAKING RIBBON BOWS

1 *Tear up strips of linen, then smear the papier mâché or flour and water paste over them. You may find this more comfortable if you wear thin disposable plastic gloves.*

2 *Now fold the outer edges in towards the centre of each strip, to give a smooth finish.*

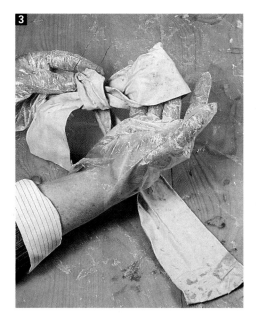

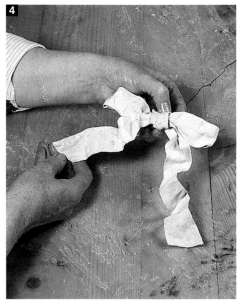

3 *Tie the linen strip into a suitable bow shape, taking care to arrange the folds and creases in a pleasing way. Thread a length of wire through the back of the bow to hold it in place in the finished design.*

4 *Make any final adjustments that you deem necessary before allowing the bow to dry. This may take several days, but it is vital that the bow should be completely dry before you begin to paint it.*

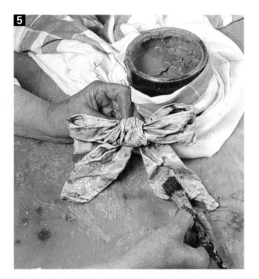

5 *Once the bow is dry, you can paint it with suitably-coloured emulsion paints. Let these dry, then cover the bow with a coat of clear matt varnish.*

Here, a painted ribbon has been used to decorate a table swag for a buffet party.

MAKING A
TOPIARY CONE

1 *Cut out a large triangle of wire netting, join the prongs of two sides together to form a conical shape and then fill with moss. Push it on to a broom handle that you have previously set in a tub filled with cement. Wire lengths of box and push them into the mossed cone, always keeping the appearance of topiary.*

2 *Here the finished topiary has been decorated with diagonal bands of roses and ribbons, but this is only one of many designs that you could create.*

CHAPTER EIGHT

TOPIARY AND TREES

As a floral decoration, the possibilities of using topiary are endless, especially when it is combined with garlands of flowers and foliage—one of my great loves. The exquisite shapes of the garlands look magnificent against the dark green foliage of the topiary.

Making topiary
You can easily make the basic shape with wet oasis, but when you plan it you must remember that the finished result will be at least 2.5cm (1in) larger all over, due to the addition of the plant material. Of course, the size of the tree will determine the number and size of oasis blocks you will need, but however many you use, they should be carved to the rough shape, staked together with green garden sticks and then covered with wire netting, which is tied or wired in place. If the design is to be large, you will need to support it with a central cane or heavy stake. Should the design need a trunk, as when making a bay tree, you will have to prepare it in advance.

Decorating the trunk
Choose an appropriately sized stick or stake, which can then be covered with ribbon or painted. However, I always like to simulate bark on these trunks, because I find it gives a better and more convincing finish. It is easy to make, though rather messy!

Smear rubber glue over the surface of the stick, then wrap lengths of cheap soft lavatory paper around it. As the paper dries, which it will do quite quickly, gently squash it and move it around a little to roughen the surface. Then paint the stick with black matt emulsion. When it is dry mix together a little brown and green emulsion to make a dirty brown, and just brush it over the surface, then use each colour separately to blend a little here and there. Allow to dry, then dip the brush into drab-coloured paint and wipe almost all of it off on to a rag or paper. Then very gently pull the brush over the surface to create the impression of weathered bark. Try again if you don't succeed at first—practice will soon make perfect. Then leave to dry.

Now choose a suitably shaped pot for the tree—an old plastic bucket or container, lined with thick plastic, will be ideal,

although a flowerpot, also lined with plastic, is a sensible and attractive choice for a tree intended to be a table decoration.

Once it is dry, place the trunk in the plastic-lined pot and fill with ready-mixed cement, then leave to set. You will now be able to remove the stick, plus its cement base, from the pot or bucket. If the plastic lining has stuck to the cement, so much the better. You can now push the block of wet oasis on to the handle and secure in place with wire—you may find this easier if you first whittle the top of the stick into a spike, using a sharp craft knife.

Choosing the foliage
The type of tree that you wish to make will affect your choice of foliage, determining its colour, shape and size, as well as type. A simple bay tree style is easily arranged by just pushing the pieces into the oasis. You can use flowers too, and the white all-year-round chrysanthemums can look very pretty and ribbon bows are also attractive. I particularly like to include little painted doves perched in the trees. One extremely useful and effective foliage to use is *Gaultheria shallon*, which is very long-lasting and a good green. Privet, euonymus and similar foliage is equally attractive, and a variety of foliage can be lovely, giving a looser style of arrangement if plant material is scarce.

A close clipped tree takes longer to make, and is best when yew, box or privet is used. An economical way in which to work is to push a stem into the oasis, then pull it out and clip it off at the required length before pushing it back into the oasis and clipping off any excess. This is not as slow a process as it first appears, and in fact is a very rewarding task. The clipped topiary tree that I made as an exhibit for a flower show lasted for many months after the event.

Using pedestals or pillars with topiary shapes is attractive, and looks even more so when the topiary is spiralled from top to bottom with garlands. Other ideas are just waiting to be created by you!

Choosing an attractive container
So far the trees only have a base made from cement, or cement and plastic, and are not

MAKING A
DECORATIVE
TREE

1 *Give a broom handle
the appearance of bark
(see p. 73), then set it
into a plastic pot filled with
ready-mix cement and
leave to dry.*

2 *Push a block of wet
oasis on to the top of the
'trunk', then cover with
wire netting and wire it
securely in place. Start
pushing the foliage into the
oasis, but do not pack it
very tightly if the foliage is
quite large.*

3 *Once all the foliage is
in place, you can decorate
the tree with painted birds
and ribbons. Place the
plastic pot in a basket and
cover the top with moss.
Alternatively, you can
place it in a terracotta pot
and arrange ivies and
plants over the cement.*

very elegant. The pots that you use for the
trees are an important part of the design
and so an ordinary plastic pot will not do!
Some very attractive terracotta pots can be
used, in which case all you need do is
carefully place the cement base in the pot,
firm it and then cover the surface of the
cement with moss, grass or a similar
material. Trailing ivies or primulas also look
charming.

Alternatively you can use the Versailles
tub—a square wooden tub, usually painted
white, with a ball set on each corner. You
can also buy very good plastic pots and
urns, but they will have to be weighted
first, with sand, lead or cement. You may
be lucky enough to find one with the ideal
colouring, but if not you can easily paint it
(*see pp. 75–80*).

Using dried foliage and flowers

Not all trees need to be made from fresh
foliage, and you can create lovely and most
interestingly-textured designs with moss,
cones, berries and fruits. These will need
similar basic mechanics, such as the trunks
and containers, but you must remember to
substitute dry brown oasis for the wet
green type. It is available in a variety of
types and shapes. Use the fine brown oasis
for small designs and the thicker, less dense
sort, for large trees.

You will have to carve the foam in the
same way, then cover with wire netting if
the arrangement is to be quite large. The
dry oasis is available in such useful shapes
as ready-formed cones and balls which will
fit on to the trunks quite easily. However,
these are only suitable for smaller trees.

Moss trees are most attractive, and
reindeer moss is particularly delightful in
shape and texture. You can buy it in either
soft or hard form but, if using the latter, it
will have to be soaked in water first. Not
only will it then be easier to use, and enable
you to remove the pine needles and any
dirty pieces, but it will also swell up to twice
its size.

Once you have made your frame, it is a
good idea to decorate and fit the container
that will be used, as these trees are not
easily transported and so the least
disturbance the better. Once the base has
been placed in the container, you can

continue. Build up the moss design piece by piece, securing the moss with wires bent double into the shape of old-fashioned hair pins. Push them down well into the oasis. If you require a very firm tree, then place a little glue on the end of each wire before pushing it into the oasis.

Lovely designs can also be made with mixtures of materials, such as dried achillea, statice, nigella, delphiniums, larkspur, grasses, poppy seed heads and wheat—the list is endless. Many of these materials are easiest to work with if they are stuck to the oasis, and a glue-gun makes this job particularly easy, with a trigger mechanism that pushes the glue sticks straight through into the oasis. Other tree designs abound using wired flowers and branches.

The trees are very useful for weddings and parties and offer endless possibilities when using ribbons, bows, berries and fruits. Even plastic fruits look good, with oranges and lemons being especially convincing. I usually paint mine to give them a more realistic appearance, although some of the plastic fruit on sale now is so lifelike it needs no improvement at all. In fact, once you begin working on trees, you'll find that time is the only restriction you'll encounter!

Painting pots and pillars

As you will have realised by now, the flower arranger soon develops many talents other than those traditionally associated with flower arranging! One particular technique that I've found very useful has been in giving my pots, pillars and pedestals a new look.

I was delighted a few years ago when such decorative paint finishes as marbling and stippling became popular. Of course, the idea is far from new, for the Greeks, Romans and Victorians were all captivated by marbled finishes. Spend some time looking at different pieces of marble and you will be amazed at their beauty.

The idea of owning pots and pedestals that looked like marble, stone and terracotta, yet could be transported easily from one place to another, appealed to me greatly, so I set about making my own. To make a pedestal or urn resemble stone is

MAKING A MOSSED TREE

1 *Find a suitable piece of gnarled vine and set it into some ready-mix cement. Here, a plastic bag has been used in place of a pot.*

2 *Securely attach a block of wet oasis, covered with wire netting, to the top of the vine. Start pinning the reindeer moss into the oasis.*

3 *Continue to add the moss. The sea lavender makes an interesting contrasting texture. Here, the base of the tree has been placed in a terracotta container and the cement covered with more moss.*

CREATING A DECORATIVE FINISH

1 *Paint the object to be marbled with black eggshell, flat oil or undercoat and leave to dry. Make up a glaze of paint and white spirit (see p. 80) and dab it over the surface.*

2 *Now flick white spirit over the wet glaze to open it up. This procedure is known as 'cissing'. Then dip a piece of crumpled newspaper in a white glaze and dab it on the black ground.*

3 *Now draw in the veins on the marble. This can be done by pulling a feather, dipped in oil paint, over the surface or, as shown here, by drawing in the veins with a wax crayon.*

4 *Diffuse the veins by drawing a large soft brush over them. Once you are pleased with the result, allow to dry thoroughly. Apply one coat of clear gloss varnish and two coats of clear matt varnish, leaving each one to dry before applying the next.*

5 *To make a stone finish, pull some drab-coloured paint gently over a painted biscuit tin. This is used in the design for the buffet table in the wedding marquee (see p. 119).*

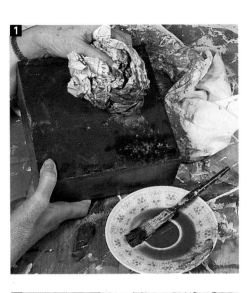

quite simple, but it does take time. However, the finished result should be ample reward.

Creating stone finishes

I have seen many efforts at painting pots, but most of them look like just that—pots that have been painted! If you want to avoid that pitfall, a good way to begin is to have a look at the real thing, or even photographs of stone pots. Immediately you will realise that stone is not made up of just one colour but many different ones. Lichen, moss, rain, snow and even grime all have their part to play in the finished texture and colouring of a piece of stone, so just buying a tin of grey paint and hoping for the best will not suffice. In fact, there may be no

Here is a smaller version of the decorative tree (see p. 74). It has been made with foliage and white daisy chrysanthemums, and has been planned as a small table decoration.

need to buy any paint specially for this job at all, as you could find that you've already got everything you need—unfinished tins of paint in almost any colour will be useful, and even children's powder paints are suitable. Plastic or fibreglass pots, urns, statues and busts all benefit wonderfully from this decorative treatment.

Start by ensuring that the pot you wish to decorate is clean and dry, then cover it with a single coat of matt emulsion and leave to dry. Use black if you want a dark finish, and white for a lighter effect. Then roughly paint the surface with a masonry paint—I used beige, because it was left over after painting our house! Choose one that will give a rough-textured finish, then allow to dry. Then, dipping your brush into first one colour and then another, such as brown, green, blue or even orange, gently paint the roughened surface. Don't slap the paint on but simply draw the brush over the surface to leave a faint residue of colour and allow to dry. Then, choosing the grey, beige or whatever stone colour you require, gently paint the whole of the pot, leaving some of the colour showing, and especially a little black in the cracks. Leave this until almost dry, then with some drab-coloured paint carefully pull the brush over the surface of the pot—it will just touch the raised parts of the paint and create a very realistic stone finish.

If you don't get quite the right result first time round, try again until you do. Each layer will give you another dimension and

This is a collection of pedestals, bases and pots that have all been given special decorative finishes that have transformed their original plastic and wooden appearances.

Facing page, *a plastic urn has been painted to resemble stone, and then used with this decorated topiary.*

help build up cracks and textures that will add character and conviction to the finished pot. On one occasion I wanted to make my pedestals and urns look very old and crackled, so I even painted in the cracks and moss, but this isn't really necessary!

Creating a terracotta finish
A terracotta finish is worked in almost the same way as a stone one, but you must omit the rough textured masonry paint because terracotta is smooth. However, the black base and undercolours are still necessary. To me, paint labelled 'terracotta' bears no resemblance to the real colour at all, and I find mixing up a variety of paint colours gives the best result. Keep an old terracotta flower pot nearby to act as instant colour reference. Once the undercoats of colour are dry, you can add a light touch of drab paint to give the lovely bloom found on real terracotta.

Creating a marbled finish
This is very impressive but equally easy to create. I once had a most enjoyable day with a friend showing her how to marble objects, and the memory of her surprise at the ease in doing so still makes me smile. Once again, the more trouble you take, the better the result will be. Over the years I have tried to make several types of marble, all of which are simple but will vary slightly. If possible, do look at the real thing because that will help you greatly.

The marble illustrated in the step-by-step photographs (*see p. 77*) is known as black serpentine marble, and is a useful colour for setting off flowers and foliage. Start by ensuring the object to be painted is clean and dry, then paint it with black eggshell, flat oil or undercoat and leave to dry. Then squeeze a very little emerald oil paint on to an old saucer, and mix in a little raw umber and black, to dirty the colour. Then mix in white spirit, at a ratio of 1:2 parts to make a glaze. Brush this over the whole object, then dip a stiff brush into the white spirit and flick it over the paint. Don't use too much or the paint will run. The aim is to leave little spots on the surface, which will open the glaze to reveal the black below—this is known as 'cissing'. Then dip a crumpled newspaper in a white glaze (made from white oil paint and white spirit mixed up in a ratio of 1:2) and dab it sparingly on the black ground.

Next, to make the veins, take a fine brush or feather and dip it in white oil paint, then gently let your hand pull the paint over the surface, twisting the brush or feather as you go. Alternatively, you can use a wax crayon. All marble veins run diagonally and should have the feeling of a meandering river, occasionally with a small tributary. Then repeat the technique in a different direction. However, don't get carried away as too few veins are better than too many! Then soften the veins by pulling a large soft brush gently over the paint in both directions. At this stage the marbling effect should be revealed. Allow to dry thoroughly before touching.

This fragile paint surface must now be varnished, not only to protect it but also to create the characteristic sheen of the real thing. Apply one coat of gloss varnish followed by two coats of matt varnish, allowing each coat to dry thoroughly before applying the next. If you wish the marble to look very old, mix an ochre tint into the final coat of varnish, but do make sure that you use it very sparingly.

Marble pedestals
My marble pedestals have been extremely useful, and I found that the only thing better than one marble pedestal was two! You can, of course, experiment with other marble colours and finishes and they can be used on anything—plastic urns, china pots, wooden bases, and so on. In fact, my friend thought about her bathroom walls, but I'm not sure that she's started them yet!

A good alternative to a pedestal, and one with which I have found it easy to work, is a box with an inbuilt stand—I persuaded a local carpenter to make several for me, and they look good whether painted as stone or marble. If painted with a stone finish, they blend in well with church arrangements. These boxes are of a useful height but can easily be made taller still by placing a container on top of the box. A plastic tray filled with simple mechanics is usually adequate. They make a very pleasing alternative to the seemingly inevitable wrought iron stand.

CHAPTER NINE

FLOWERS AS GIFTS

Flowers make wonderful presents, whether as pot plants or arrangements. However, as with other gifts, your presentation can play a major part in the recipient's joy, and because flowers are living, it is especially important to ensure that they are prepared and packed properly. (It would be a great disappointment to receive bruised or battered flowers.) They therefore need to be easily transported, easily maintained and given firm mechanics. The container will also have to be chosen carefully, whether it is part of the gift itself or just a means of presenting the flowers.

Using baskets

There are many pretty baskets that make a good choice for a gift, as they are easy to handle and can be used again afterwards. Plastic trays are often used too, and simple china containers are relatively inexpensive. If you are planning a very special present, then you can be as extravagant as you wish!

A gift that has been carefully planned for someone has a special significance. This basket of spring flowers – daffodils, narcissi and muscari – was planned to match the John Parkinson prints on the wall behind.

PRESENTING A FLOWER

1 *Wire up some fern leaves, then carefully push a wire through the stem of an orchid.*

2 *Tape the ferns and the orchid stem together and push a decorative pin through the stem if the orchid is to be worn as a corsage.*

3 *Place a block of crumpled tissue paper in a presentation box, carefully place the orchid spray on top and then complete with an attractive velvet bow.*

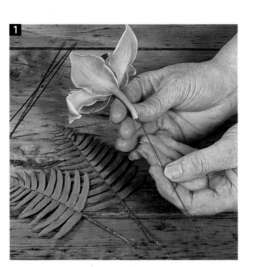

WRAPPING A BOUQUET IN CELLOPHANE

1 *Place a long length of cellophane on a flat surface. Arrange the bouquet in the centre of the cellophane, then carefully draw the rest of the cellophane over the bouquet.*

2 *Separate the cellophane from the remainder of the roll, then turn under the two cut sides and staple them together. Gather the cellophane around the stems of the bouquet, ensuring that the flower heads are not being squashed or crushed, then fasten with a large ribbon in a colour that matches the flowers.*

Cut flowers arranged in baskets are very popular and follow the normal arrangements in this style, but you will have to secure a plastic liner into the container.

It can sometimes be a problem to hide the mechanics when using plastic trays and small dishes, but pinning leaves or some small pieces of conifer over the oasis will help. The simpler your design for this sort of arrangement, the more effective it will be, especially if you use variegated ivies, euphorbias and other interesting material.

Presentation bouquets

Presentation bouquets and posies vary tremendously, depending on the flowers used and the particular occasion for which they are intended, but they are always much appreciated and look quite beautiful if properly presented. It must be said that presentation bouquets or boxes of cut flowers can be very expensive—unless you are fortunate enough to be able to pick all the material from your garden—so if you have to work to a tight budget I would strongly suggest that you choose a few really beautiful flowers rather than masses of cheaper ones. Don't forget to add some foliage, preferably choosing something unusual or particularly decorative.

Cut flowers look lovely when carefully placed in a cellophane box and tied up with ribbon to keep the lid in place. Choose a ribbon with a soft sheen for a better finish—there is a wonderful ribbon with wire running through the edges which looks lovely when tied, but it is quite expensive. An elegant card with a clearly written message adds the perfect finishing touch.

Presents for patients

Flower gifts for hospitals are very special,

Filling a decorative container with a pot plant makes a perfect present for Mothers' Day.

MAKING A SMALL POSY

1 *Wire up individual flowers, and then tape their stems with stem tape – you can split this in two for a neater finish when working with small flowers.*

2 *Assemble the posy by taping all the stems together to form an attractive design. A decorative frill around the edge of the posy gives a neat finish. This sort of posy is a lovely gift for a female guest at a dinner party.*

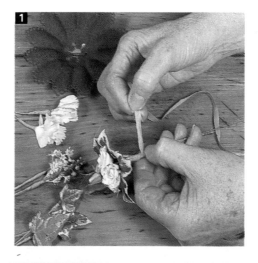

MAKING A
HOSTESS POSY

1 *A hostess posy is
arranged in the hand and
then securely bound with
stem tape. Bind the stems
together as you add them,
crossing the stems as you
work. Then cut the stems
level, cover the posy with
cellophane and place more
cellophane over the stems,
add a little water to keep
the flowers fresh, then
secure firmly with ribbon.*

2 *Once the cellophane
wrapping has been
removed the posy needs no
further arranging but can
be placed in water as it is.
This makes it an ideal gift
for people who don't have
the time or the facility to
arrange the flowers
themselves.*

and you can choose from any of the ideas
given here. Arranged flowers, however,
are often one of the most practical ideas,
especially if they have already been placed
in oasis. One lovely idea for people who are
convalescing at home is to fill shells with
flowers, as they always look pretty and the
shell itself can be kept in the bathroom
afterwards, filled with silk or dried flowers.

Flowers for babies
Gifts to celebrate the arrival of a new baby
are always a great pleasure to make and
there is a whole host of ideas from which to
choose. Basket designs are charming when
made in a variety of shapes, and especially
prams. When choosing flowers for babies,
anything pretty and delicate is most
effective, particularly when combined with
sprays of small-leaved foliage.

Flowering bulbs
Planted and flowering bulbs are particularly
acceptable on cold winter days, and they
give a lovely foretaste of the spring to

come. If you don't want to grow your own bulbs you can buy them instead. Sometimes they are grown in grass, which looks very attractive and natural.

Once again, presentation is important, and you will have to pay some attention to your choice of container. Baskets and bulbs have a tremendous affinity, and really cannot be bettered, although of course you will have to line them with black plastic first, ensuring that the soil line does not reach the top of the basket. Moss also looks attractive when used to cover the soil. I have seen small stones placed in the top of

pots or baskets, but I always find that they get spilled over the edges. The choice of bulbs is very varied, so unless you know that your recipient loves a particular flower, try to choose plants that are unusual or rare.

The list of gift ideas is endless, with Christmas, birthdays, Valentine's Day, Easter and wedding anniversaries just some of the occasions that can be celebrated with flowers. The most important element, I feel, is the choice of plant materials within the design. The more varied and interesting they are, the more pleasure you will give.

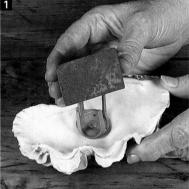

MAKING A SHELL ARRANGEMENT

1 *Find a suitable shell with a fairly flat base. Fix a small frog to the interior and add a small piece of wet oasis. These must be firm as the gift will have to be transported.*

2 *Now add the flowers, ensuring that the size of the arrangement is in keeping with that of the shell. You must also check that the flowers hide all the mechanics, which may be visible if the shell is very shallow.*

This little wheelbarrow filled with fresh flowers makes an unusual present for a keen gardener.

Little wicker prams filled with flowers are a refreshingly different way of celebrating the birth of a baby.

CHAPTER TEN

POT-ET-FLEUR AND ARRANGING WITH HOUSEPLANTS

If you live in a part of the world where you cannot always guarantee to have a wealth of fresh flowers at your disposal, do not despair, for a little lateral thinking may work wonders. For example, combining pot plants and flowers, known as *pot-et-fleur*, is a very practical and elegant idea and may well save the day if you're racking your brains for inspiration when faced with the minimum of fresh plant material. The plants will combine their variety and interest with splashes of colour from the flowers. They will also give you a living arrangement which will be a joy for many weeks to come.

Creating *pot-et-fleur* arrangements is very rewarding, and the contrasts of foliage and colour can be stunning. Experimenting, particularly with different flowers, will reveal the wealth of possibilities available to you. These arrangements are especially suitable for offices, entrance halls and other such areas, and are ideal for people who don't have gardens. They are also a boon to the busy housewife who wants a floral decoration in case an unexpected visitor arrives, and in addition they make ideal and attractive gifts.

Whichever plants you choose, they will have to be fed and watered regularly, just like other pot plants. They'll settle together surprisingly quickly, for they seem to enjoy each other's company. The plant arrangement will be at its best a week or two after it has been planted—worth remembering if you need the arrangement for a special occasion.

Choosing the right pot plants

It is important to spend time choosing the pot plants you will use in your arrangement, because they will all have to live together in harmony, sharing the same needs for light, heat and moisture. Disaster will surely strike if you combine a plant that thrives in full sun with one that only likes deep shade! If you are worried about choosing compatible plants yourself, then don't be afraid to ask the person who sells them to you, or check their requirements in a good gardening book before visiting a shop or garden centre.

Firstly, decide where the plants will be positioned, then choose the types

accordingly. It will help if all the plants need the same amounts of water, unless you intend to spend a great deal of time nursing each one individually!

The foliage should also be as varied in shape and texture as possible, so exercise the same care that you would when choosing flowers for an arrangement, ensuring that the plants have a variety in height and downward flow. This is probably more important than the choice of colour, although of course this must be considered because it will be a very dull arrangement indeed if all your plants are the same colour. If you will be buying all the pot plants at the same time, ask if they can be grouped together to give you some idea of their finished appearance.

Finding a suitable container

You should also pay careful thought to your choice of container, and it must be of such a depth that there will be a gap of about 2.5cm (1in) below the rim once the largest plant has been placed in position. This will ensure that none of the potting compost is washed out whenever you water the plants. Such containers as Victorian wash bowls and copper preserving pans are ideal, but whatever you choose, first ensure good drainage by placing a layer of gravel in the base of the container.

Planting the arrangement without pots

I prefer to remove the plants from their pots before positioning them in the container, but it is not absolutely necessary. If you will be removing the pot, tap it gently on one side then carefully pull it away from the soil, keeping the root ball intact while supporting the stem. Place a layer of good-quality potting compost over the drainage gravel, then arrange all the plants on top of this compost until you are happy with their positions. Fill in the gaps with more compost, firming it around the plants, until it is 2.5cm (1in) below the rim. Not every plant has the same sized root ball, so you may have to place more compost beneath smaller plants so that they are not planted below their natural soil lines. When planting, remember to leave some space for the flower container.

Planting the arrangement with pots
Plants without their pots seem to blend together more naturally in these arrangements, but there are advantages to keeping them in their pots. Firstly, it is easy to change them about, especially if one of the plants fails or is looking unhappy. Secondly, if the plants have different soil or moisture requirements you will be making life a lot easier by keeping them in their separate pots.

Place the pots directly on to the gravel, arrange them to your taste, then fill in the gaps with peat. You can cover this with moss, but you must still leave a gap of at least 2.5cm (1in) between the compost and the rim of the container. The plants will enjoy these growing conditions, but do remember to keep them moist as the peat and moss absorb plenty of water.

An alternative to keeping the plants in pots is to wrap the root ball of each one in thin polythene (small polythene food bags are a good choice), adding plenty of potting compost, before planting. This prevents the root systems becoming tangled up in each other once they are growing in the container and therefore you will still find it easy to change the plants around whenever necessary. Again, when arranging the plants, remember to leave enough space for the flower container.

This pot of daisies and ivy was inspired by the illustration by Ehret in the bottom left of the photograph. Ehret was a major figure in the science of botany.

Choosing the flowers and their container

This should be reasonably deep—a medium-sized plant pot is usually about right. (Don't use a flower pot as the water will drain away through the hole in the base!) Fit a pin-holder in the base and perhaps a little wire netting to hold the flowers in place. Then position the container so that its rim extends 2.5–5cm (1–2in) above the compost level—this helps to prevent any of the compost finding its way into the water and will also make it easier for you to top it up with water.

Adding the flowers

By now you should have a balanced arrangement of plants which will give you height, interest, depth and focal point, whether or not you add any flowers. This will enable you to enjoy the arranged plants at all times, and you can then add the flowers for extra interest. You will find that the flowers from varying seasons will create varying effects, although the bold and dramatic flowers will always give a more pleasing result. Lilies, daffodils, irises, orchids, gladioli and gerberas all look effective, but never include too many because a few simply arranged flowers are usually quite adequate. You can give extra height if necessary with a cone, but always keep everything in proportion, and don't let the flowers overwhelm the plants. As the flower container is not very large you will have to top it up with water at frequent intervals. If you do use a cone, that will also have to be topped up with water as necessary.

Adding bulbs and driftwood

Bulbs which have been forced in pots also look very attractive with an arrangement of plants, with the bulb pot taking the place of the flower container. It can easily be removed once the flowers have faded. Hyacinths, daffodils and narcissi look particularly effective.

Driftwood is another lovely foil for pot plants and gives an added dimension to the design. It can be pushed on to a pin-holder for stability or just gently placed in the arrangement, allowing it to be removed more easily.

CREATING POT-ET-FLEUR

1 *Place a layer of gravel, followed by one of potting compost, in the pan. Gently knock the largest plant out of its pot and arrange it in the pan first.*

2 *Now add the rest of the plants, placing them horizontally or vertically as your design dictates. Fill the flower container with some wet oasis and wire netting and position it in the pan.*

3 *Here, the finished design is shown, with contrasting plants and foliage used to good effect. The lilies, which have been chosen as the fresh flowers, are long-lasting.*

CHAPTER ELEVEN

FLOWERS FOR PLACES OF WORSHIP

Church flowers are probably the most obvious examples of the flower arranger's talents. The very size involved gives greater scope and there is tremendous enjoyment to be gained from making arrangements for such festivities as Easter, Harvest Festivals, Christmas, weddings, christenings and even funerals. In fact, I feel that funeral flowers are often overlooked, with the exception of wreaths and tributes, which is a great shame because this really is a time when flowers can bring great comfort.

I suppose the first consideration when working with arrangements for churches, synagogues and other places of worship is their size, which can be rather daunting after doing flowers for the home. If you are about to arrange some church flowers for the first time, then take heart—the basic principles of floral design will still apply, but the materials you use will have to be bolder. You will also have to assess the style of the place of worship, ensuring that your arrangements are in keeping with it. Ornate churches and similar buildings need simple yet elegant arrangements, while modern buildings call for uncluttered designs.

If you own a pair of altar vases they can make very attractive decorations for the home. Here, the vases have been filled with sand to give stability, and then wet oasis has been placed in their tops and secured with fine tape. This allows the flowers to flow down, thereby creating a more attractive design.

MAKING AN ALTAR ARRANGEMENT

1 *As it is important to create this arrangement in* situ, *you must protect the altar cloth with a large table cloth or something similar. Set the mechanics slightly behind the crucifix and then create the outline.*

2 *Continue to build up the design, allowing the lilies to create the form that will be taken. Take care not to distract attention from the crucifix – keeping the flowers low may help.*

3 *Here, the finished design is shown. The gold-coloured roses were chosen to continue the theme and colouring of the altar cloth.*

MAKING A PEW
END DESIGN

1 *This plastic holder
containing oasis is a
proprietary pew end
mechanic that can easily
be fitted over the pew. It is
re-usable.*

2 *Now add the plant
material, starting with the
foliage. It is important to
ensure that you have
obscured all the
mechanics.*

MAKING A PEW END DESIGN

1 *This is an alternative plastic pew end holder that is used once and then thrown away. It is useful because it can be used in several positions. Here, it is seen in the longest position, ready for a long, slender floral design.*

2 *Now add the foliage and flowers, creating an elegant, draped effect. It is not always desirable to decorate every pew end, as the finished result may look very fussy. To avoid this, you could decorate every second or third pew end for a more restful feeling.*

DECORATING A PILLAR

1 *This pillar has been decorated with a painted basket that would be equally suitable for a pew end – the ribbons would just hook over the pew. In this instance the basket has been painted to match the pillar, but if it were being used for a pew end then it would be preferable to colour it the same shade as the wood.*

2 *Once lined with plastic and filled with wet oasis, the basket can be filled with a simple but elegant design using the minimum of plant material. If used for a wedding, the ribbons could match the overall colour scheme.*

Probably the most effective arrangement for any such place is a massed design with a well-defined outline, and you should always aim for a sense of dignity and calm.

Many people tend to think that flowers and flower arrangements are unnecessary in places of worship, believing that the buildings themselves are beautiful enough not to need any additional decoration. Admittedly, sometimes one can hardly see the architecture for all the floral decorations, which is something I dislike—flowers should enhance, not hide! However, I cannot imagine a wedding without flowers, Easter without lilies, Harvest Festivals without fruits and vegetables, nor the porch without a floral welcome.

Using existing containers

Most places of worship have their own containers, although occasionally I despair at some of the pots that are available! I also have a great dislike of wrought iron pedestals. I know they are useful, but there are so many other more interesting ideas that could be used instead. If, however, you are stuck with the inevitable brass vase, which usually has flowers just stuffed into it, try placing oasis and wire netting in the top so that you can create a downward-flowing design. The wrought iron pedestal looks less stark if ivies and similar foliage are allowed to trail down over it. Large leaves covering the front of the container and a deliberately soft outline will help to prevent the 'surprised hedgehog' appearance of so many of these designs!

Working tidily

It is essential that you clear up after arranging the flowers in a place of worship, and you will find life much easier if you work with a florist's dust sheet in place (*see p. 46*), as with luck that will have collected all the rubbish, and all you need to do is pick it up by its handles and depart. If there will be a lot of rubbish, then large plastic refuse bags are invaluable. A dustpan and brush should be part of your usual equipment, but if not, do remember to take them with you on this occasion—I always find that if there are any on the premises they are bound to have been locked in the caretaker's cupboard!

MAKING A WINDOW ARRANGEMENT

1 *Church windows are often very difficult to decorate because they frequently slope downwards. Here, wooden wedges have been placed beneath the container to make it level and secure. Create the basic outline with light plant material.*

2 *Place the heavier flowers in the centre of the design to give a good focal point. This arrangement shows off the shape of the window to good advantage without smothering it, while allowing the view to still be visible to the congregation.*

MAKING A BASKET
ARRANGEMENT FOR A WINDOW

1 *Line an attractive basket with plastic and fill with wet oasis, then place on the window ledge. Create the outline with light plant material.*

2 *Complete the arrangement by adding the flowers. As well as being an interesting window arrangement, this basket can also be taken to a sick member of the congregation.*

DECORATING A FONT

1 *Arrangements to decorate a font can vary in many ways. Here, oasis packs have been wired to the font and the basic outline created with cow parsley. If you use this, do make sure it has been properly conditioned otherwise it will droop very quickly.*

2 *Complete the arrangement, keeping to the colour scheme of soft creams and whites that is so suitable for a christening. It is important to give some depth to this arrangement, as otherwise it will look very solid.*

Making the most of the building

Window ledges in churches, synagogues, mosques and the like can sometimes cause problems, especially if they slope down without a level position for your container. You can solve this by wiring a wooden wedge on to the ledge, thereby giving you a flat area for your dish or tray. Remember it is never easy to work against the light, and heavier leaves and flowers will show up best when silhouetted against a window. You can add some lighter sprays to soften the overall effect.

The font is always a lovely position for flowers, particularly for a christening or baptism. Blocks of oasis can be arranged on the top or sides and filled with flowers for a very pretty arrangement. However, if you will be decorating the building for a christening, you should first check with the priest as you may not be allowed to decorate the font itself, or may be limited as to size. If that's the case, candle arrangements are a lovely alternative.

Very often, places of worship hold festivals of flowers, so do help out if you are asked. As I have already mentioned, the prime consideration is to ensure that the building will still be visible once the flowers are in place, so don't smother all the architecture with volumes of flowers! It is always a matter of courtesy to consult the priest before creating arrangements in a place of worship that is unfamiliar to you, particularly when you will be decorating the altar—some priests have very definite views on the subject. If they are allowed, then ask about their position and size and ensure you stick to the guidelines.

Many religious buildings have beautiful pillars, and there are some lovely ways in which to decorate them. They are also very useful since they will be visible to the congregation whether they are standing or seated. Swags always look elegant and can be used to great effect on special occasions. Garlands arranged around pillars also look attractive.

Working with pedestals

Pedestals are usually placed by the altar and at the entrance to the building, and usually look most effective if they are all arranged with similar, but not identical, plant material

and foliage. This will give the impression of a thoughtful design and form a harmonious link between each pedestal arrangement.

As a rule, the whole of the pedestal will be on view, so you will have to ensure that its back is just as decorative as its front. This will mean you have to take care when planning the outline. A good starting point is the design using seven stems (*see pp. 18–22*), taking care to remember the back of the arrangement. Trailing and flowing ivies and branches help to stop the feeling of the arrangement being cut off. Large leaves, such as *Bergenia cordifolia*, are useful for the front, but don't let them hang down too far as they can give the appearance of thirsty dogs! Placing the largest and brightest flowers on the focal point will also help, particularly when the arrangement is viewed from a distance. Once you have worked on these designs you will realise that they are just as easy as those created at home on a smaller scale—they simply need more impressive materials.

Although I always advocate arranging flowers *in situ*, this is especially important when working on pedestals for places of worship. So many arrangers opt to do their flowers at home in a vase of their own, and then place or tie it in position when they arrive at their destination. This is convenient for them but doesn't produce nearly such a pleasing arrangement.

Easter flowers

This is a lovely time to arrange flowers in a place of worship. After the absence of flowers and the sombre feeling through Lent they look wonderfully alive and vivid. Yellow is a marvellously uplifting colour and is perfect for this festival, particularly when combined with the analagous colourings of green and cream. I can never understand why brides choose pink or apricot flowers at this time of the year!

Daffodils, narcissi and similar flowers are not always easy to arrange, but try placing the heads in different directions and varying the heights a little. If you are using oasis, you will have to cut the stems at a good sharp angle and make small holes in the oasis first with a knitting needle, otherwise the stems will become bent and useless. Wire netting may be a much more viable

The deep colours of this simple window design make it a good choice for a funeral, and it would look very effective in a porch, to greet the mourners as they arrive for the service.

alternative, or you can buy special oasis for these sorts of flower. Arums and longiflorum lilies are ideal for Easter arrangements, particularly for the altar (if that is allowed), using only just enough foliage to cover the mechanics.

For me, one of the most important places in which to arrange flowers is the porch, as they give a lovely welcome to everyone who enters the building. Keeping things simple is best, and just a basket of primulas or daffodils can look absolutely charming.

Harvest and Thanksgiving flowers
Harvest Festivals are a super excuse for a riot of colour, and the combination of flowers, fruits, vegetables, berries and seeds makes it a marvellous time of extravagance in colour and design. I remember going to a Harvest Festival service years ago in which every window ledge had been lovingly and painstakingly covered with alternate green apples and red tomatoes. It must have taken hours but produced such a magnificent effect that I still remember it with pleasure.

Swags are very effective at this time of year, especially if you make them from fruits and berries. Some of the plastic fruit that is available can also be put to good use here. Unfortunately, attaching the swags can sometimes cause a problem, and although ideally they should be hung from nails already hammered into the pillar, this isn't always possible. Rather than start banging nails into the pillar, wind wires around them instead, which will be just as effective and far less drastic.

Choose vibrant, glowing colours for this time of the year—sprays of berries, *Clematis vitalba*, blackberries, seed pods and crab apples all add texture and dimension, and their marvellous colourings and sheens instantly create the right atmosphere. The autumnal colourings of foliage are themselves a joy and can give great pleasure. A lovely altar arrangement can be made from wheat, lilies and grapes, and a design incorporating the harvest loaf, wheat, grapes and fruit is a classic feature in many places of worship in the autumn.

Christmas
This is surely one of the most joyous occasions of the year, when you have every

DECORATING PEDESTALS

1 *Assemble the mechanics for the pedestals and place them in position. Create a soft flowing outline with the plant material, remembering to include pieces that trail down quite low in the design.*

2 *Do not forget to decorate the back of each pedestal as well as the front. Here, one of the pedestals has been turned around to show its decoration.*

3 *Complete the design by filling in with more flowers. The two pedestals are used here to frame the altar. Their designs are similar, but not exactly alike, which gives them greater interest and style.*

DECORATING A PILLAR

1 *This is always a lovely idea, and as the designs are high up they are easily visible for all the congregation, whether standing or seated. Tie oasis 'sausages' (see pp. 66–7) around the ledge of the pillar and cover the mechanics with a little foliage. This can be inserted before the garland of oasis is put in position.*

2 *Complete the arrangement by adding flowers and more foliage if necessary. Here, pretty pieces of trailing ivy help to soften the arrangement and carry one's eye down the pillar.*

MAKING A HARVEST ARRANGEMENT

1 *As always, it is very important to create this arrangement* in situ. *The position of this design means that the congregation and choir will have to move around it, in which case there must not be any trailing pieces over which anyone could trip. Here, the harvest sheaf, cornucopia and dried corn are all in harmony with the stone pedestal.*

2 *Build up the design with flowers, foliage, fruits and vegetables. Here, cauliflowers, beans, tomatoes, peppers, carrots and mushrooms and a plaited harvest loaf have been incorporated into the design, with lilies, poppies and white daisy chrysanthemums. Dahlias and Michaelmas daisies would also be very suitable. If berries are to be used they will last longer if lacquered first. Lacquering also helps to prevent bulrushes and fluffy grasses shedding their seeds.*

excuse for creating magnificently extravagant arrangements. There seem to be two schools of thought as far as Christmas colour is concerned, with arrangements being either all-white or all-red. I love them both! When working with all-white arrangements, I find that adding a few red berries to the holly creates a lovely feel—wire on artificial ones if the holly doesn't have any. There are many wonderful foliages from which to choose for added interest, such as elaeagnus and the spotted laurels. Red arrangements just glow, and deep green and grey foliages are perfect partners.

Funerals
Once you become proficient and well-known for your ecclesiastical flower arrangements, you may well be asked to arrange the flowers for funerals, and if you've never done so before you could find it a daunting prospect at first. However, there will be no need to worry if you follow these guidelines.

At a funeral there is always a sad and quiet time before the service begins, and beautiful flowers can create a calm and comforting atmosphere, particularly if the coffin or casket has already been placed in the chapel. Two low pedestals positioned on either side can look lovely, especially if they match the colourings of the family flowers. If this isn't practical or possible, you can match the flowers to the colourings in the church instead. An arrangement placed in the porch or entrance is always appreciated (as long as it doesn't get in the way) and can help to lighten what is often a very sombre atmosphere.

You may be asked to make a wreath or floral tribute for the funeral, and this is an especially important commission. The family, in particular, will want it to be a beautiful expression of their love, so it should show sympathy and thoughtfulness, often using favourite flowers or colourings. Ideally, you should also use suitable flowers, perhaps choosing bold ones for a man, more delicate flowers for a woman and small, pretty material for a child. Using interesting foliage is just as important for funeral work as it is for any other type of flower arranging, and it will also help to

MAKING A CHRISTMAS ARRANGEMENT

1 *Place a large mould on a candlestick and wedge oasis into it. Make the outline of the design with flowing ivy and variegated holly.*

2 *Very often berries are missing from holly, in which case you can wire on a few artificial ones to help create a festive feeling.*

3 *Add some red flowers to complete the design – red spray carnations were used here. A pair of candlesticks ranged either side of the altar would look very beautiful.*

create the impression that you really cared about what you were doing.

There are many styles of funeral tributes, but here I have chosen three of the most popular examples: a simple wreath on a wired frame; a cross made on an oasis frame; and a funeral bunch.

Making a simple wreath

Wreaths can be made in a variety of sizes, using wire frames that are sold ready-assembled. If the wreath is to be very large it can be placed on a stand at the funeral.

Firstly, the frame is covered with moss. This will form the foundation for the flowers, so it is important that it is as firm as possible—if you do not do this, the flowers will fall out.

To cover the frame you will need plenty of moist moss (bought in bags) and a roll of fine green garden twine. Knot the end of the garden twine on to the frame, then take a large handful of moss, place it on the frame and bind it in place with the twine, winding it round and round until it is firm. Do not cut it! Then cover the next piece of wire framework with moss and bind it in place. Continue in this way until the whole of the frame is covered with a firm layer of moss and the wreath is a good shape. Once you are happy with it, secure and cut the twine, then trim off any loose moss with a pair of scissors, taking care not to cut the twine in the process. Pin leaves to the underside, overlapping them to give a neat appearance.

Each flower will have to be wired before being placed in position, and to do this you must make a hair pin shape with stub wire, ensuring that one end is longer than the other. Then hold the flower stem and hair pin firmly, and wind the longer wire around the shorter one two or three times, ensuring that you enclose the flower stem in the wire. The legs will now be the same length and can easily be inserted in the moss. Sometimes the wire can be pushed through the stem before being made into the hair pin and then twisted around the stem.

This wreath design looks lovely when filled with many pretty flowers and unusual or decorative foliage.

MAKING A PEDESTAL FOR A FUNERAL

1 *Choose two low pedestals, to be positioned either side of the coffin. Create the basic outline, keeping the design simple.*

2 *Continue to build up the design. Here, hydrangea plants have been used, with all the soil washed from each plant's roots before being placed in a plastic bag with some water. Each one was securely tied to a stick and then placed in the design.*

3 *Complete the arrangement, adding flowers and some trailing foliage to soften the effect. The colours chosen here are strong but sympathetic.*

MAKING A WIRED FUNERAL WREATH

1 *Bind some damp moss on to a wire wreath frame, using soft green garden twine, until it is completely covered.*

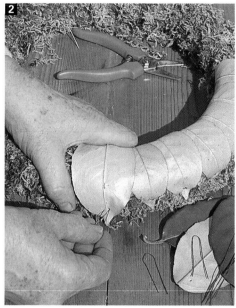

2 *Pin leaves of* Elaeagnus × ebbingei *around the back to form a neat backing. Bend stub wires into the shapes of hair pins and use these to hold the leaves in place.*

3 *Now begin to wire the flowers for the design and insert them in the moss.*

4 *Complete the design with more flowers. Spray the wreath with a fine mist of water if it is not to be used immediately.*

MAKING AN OASIS CROSS

1 *As well as wire frames, you can also buy special shapes made from oasis. Here, an oasis cross, with a plastic backing, has been chosen, damped down with water and then 'greened' with foliage to give an attractive background. Add a dome-shaped piece of oasis to the centre of the cross for extra height, or buy a proprietary device that screws into place.*

2 *Now add different types of foliage to add interest and variety.*

3 *Begin to arrange the flowers, using the heightened piece of oasis as the centre of the floral design.*

4 *It is important to choose flowers that will form a good and visible contrast with the foliage, so that they stand out both during the ceremony and afterwards.*

Making a cross

Crosses can be made in a variety of sizes, and you should be able to find an oasis framework in a size suitable for your needs. These frames usually have a plastic backing, which makes them very simple to use. It is easy to soak the oasis frame before using it, but take care not to make it too wet otherwise it will just crumble when you start to insert the flowers.

The frame must first be 'greened'—covered with foliage. This can easily be done by pushing pieces of cupressus into the oasis and then pinning them down. A mixed foliage base also looks attractive. The floral design can then be easily worked to give a feeling of depth and shape.

Making a funeral bunch

Funeral bunches are often planned with the idea of sending the flowers on to a hospital once the funeral is over. However, I don't think they are often used in this way and I'm not certain that hospitals like to receive funeral flowers anyway.

A funeral bunch is made quite easily using about three dozen flowers and some foliage—eucalyptus is a good choice. To make a bunch, take the largest piece of foliage and a roll of green garden twine, and tie the twine to the foliage. Then, take the largest spray of flowers and tie them into the foliage. Continue tying the flowers and foliage in piece by piece, working from the largest through to the shortest and always ensuring that the twine is in the same position and bound in the same direction, otherwise the plant material will slip out of place. Keep an eye on the design as you work. Once all the flowers and foliage have been bound in position, fasten off the twine securely and hide it with tape or a pretty ribbon bow.

As well as weddings, christenings, funerals and all the special dates in the ecclesiastical calendar, some flower clubs and societies also hold flower festivals for fund raising. However, the main work goes on week in, week out, with the floral decoration of churches, synagogues, mosques, chapels and cathedrals everywhere, giving us time to 'consider the lilies of the field'.

MAKING A FUNERAL BUNCH

1 *Floral tributes are often preferred at funerals and do allow the flowers to be used afterwards, if wished. Here, the greenery and tallest flowers are tied together with soft green garden twine.*

2 *Begin to add more flowers and greenery, tying them in place as you work and keeping the bunch a good shape. It is important to always bind them in the same place, otherwise the flowers will slip about when carried.*

3 *Once you are happy with the bunch, secure the twine before severing it from the roll. Tie a length of ribbon around the stems to hide the twine and finish with a large bow.*

4 *The finished bunch, showing the way in which all the flowers and foliage are visible.*

CHAPTER TWELVE

WEDDINGS

'The wedding has been announced . . .' Those words immediately start a flurry of excitement that usually continues unabated until the great day itself. If you are asked to help arrange the flowers for the wedding, do say 'yes'. It really is the most exciting and enjoyable experience!

Drawing up a plan of campaign
Your first priority is to meet the bride, so that you can assess her personality, style, taste and appearance. All these points will be invaluable when you begin to plan the wedding flowers.

Astonishingly enough, although it is the bride's day, very often her wishes are not considered in the ideas and plans, so it is important for you to talk to her as soon as possible. She may want her mother, or a close friend or relative, to be there as well. Go along armed with a notebook and pen, so that you can jot down all the essential information. If you are not told everything you need to know, then don't be afraid to ask! For example, you will need to know the date and time of the wedding, the venue, ideas for colour schemes and so on. You should also check on your level of involvement if you're not absolutely certain of what you're expected to do—far better to sort it all out at an early stage than discover at the last minute that you're supposed to do twice the amount of work that you envisaged! Do remember that the preparation of a wedding can be a very

Planning a wedding is very important and often quite time-consuming, but nevertheless it is good fun to work towards such a joyous occasion. Sketches of the dresses, wedding cake and photographs of the wedding venue are all a great help when designing the floral arrangements.

tiring, as well as an exciting, time, and wires have been known to become crossed before now!

There are four main questions that you should ask:

1 What are the dates, times and venues, and when will you be able to decorate and, later, to clear?

2 What are the preferred colourings and does the bride have any favourite flowers or, equally, are there any that she hates?

3 Will the wedding be grand, simple or otherwise, and what will your budget be?

4 Will other help be available to you?

Once you have taken all the notes you need, go home and ponder on them, then try to visit whichever venues you will be concerned with. Put your ideas down on paper and, if possible, work out some preliminary colour schemes. Then arrange another meeting, during which you can discuss your ideas and sort out any changes of plan. Try not to leave any loose ends, unless they are absolutely unavoidable, as the family will have plenty to arrange themselves and will be delighted if they know that you're getting on with your job without recourse to constant consultations or endless questions about things you've already discussed together. Nevertheless, it is far better to check anything you are unsure of, rather than forge full steam ahead and discover too late that you've made a mistake!

The bride will naturally be anxious, and in particular about the bouquets, posies and head dresses, and these will all have to be discussed once the dress designs and colour schemes have been established. Simple drawings and diagrams do help, and you don't have to be a professional artist to indicate line and shape. I often take photographs of the wedding and reception venues and then sketch my designs on the photographs to give the bride a better visual idea of what I've planned.

Weddings are a time for rejoicing and there is often a tendency to get carried away by the occasion. (Well, it happens to me, anyway!) Remember that this is a service, not a flower festival, and although it goes without saying that you should do a good job, it isn't necessarily a time to show off all your expertise! Do abide by the golden rule that flowers should enhance and not hide. Another helpful consideration is the colouring, and it is helpful to remember that once the guests arrive there will be an explosion of colour from their clothes.

Experience has proved that many time-consuming ideas, which look marvellous on paper, will be completely lost when the congregation are standing. Of course, I'm not suggesting that all the arrangements should be above eye-level, but do bear in mind that it will look rather bleak if no flowers are visible for most of the service. Decorating pillars and window sills can solve this problem, and pew end designs, which are always attractive, can look very pretty if raised up on stands.

Planning the flowers for the ceremony
The porch, entrance hall or church gate, if there is one, is a good starting point for your designs. Not only will it be a lovely welcome, but it will also set the colour scheme. Swags, garlands or little trees are delightful when arranged around the gate, but don't make them so large that they impede progress, catch on the guests' clothes or swiftly become bald because everyone brushes against them! A basket arrangement looks very pretty in the porch or entrance, and can be a gift for the mother-in-law afterwards. A second placement as you enter the place of worship or room itself will help to establish the colour scheme and give greater impact.

The altar should be the focal point for the decoration and planned accordingly. Don't use too many flowers, as large simple designs look so much more elegant than many small fussy ideas. Pew end designs are pretty, and arrangements on window sills, pillar swags and garlands are all a delight, but not if you have all of them at the same time! Beauty and dignity are the keywords to remember and a stunning arrangement on either side of the altar is sometimes all that is required.

Ribbons aren't my preference in places of

Don't neglect the importance of attractive arrangements to greet the wedding guests on their arrival at the reception (facing page). *Not only do they look lovely in their own right, but they also create a festive atmosphere and help to break the ice by providing a topic of conversation, should one be needed. This is a massed arrangement suitable for a hall or hotel fireplace.*

worship but if you do want to use them you must take great care in choosing the right sort. The very shiny stiff bows are best for parties or the reception, but you can buy very good soft ribbons with a duller finish that look very convincing. Alternatively, if the budget allows, you can splash out on very expensive ribbons. If it is available, you can make up bows using fabric from the dress of the bride, matron of honour or bridesmaid, and they will look particularly elegant if intertwined with ivies and allowed to trail on the floor as pew end designs.

Planning the flowers for the reception
Wedding receptions are held in so many different settings that it is almost impossible to cover all eventualities. Nevertheless, on the following pages I shall give you a few basic ideas that can be adapted in a number of different ways.

The type of reception that is to be held will determine your flower requirements, and a set wedding breakfast or buffet will take a lot of planning. Less formal receptions call for a different, more relaxed approach. The decoration and position of the wedding cake, always an important focal point, will also have to be considered, whether it is placed on the top table, on a table by itself or as part of the buffet. The bride may want the base of the cake to be decorated with flowers, garlands around the table or a floral arrangement placed on the top tier of the cake itself.

Camouflaging problem areas
Church and local halls are often chosen for receptions, but they can cause many problems when it comes to decorating them. Usually they are painted in dreary colours and often have very dull furniture. Don't panic if you are faced with a similar situation, because there are several quick and easy solutions to the problem. Most important of all, you should aim to detract the eye from the bad points and focus on the wedding party instead who will look good. Trying to hide a fire extinguisher behind a beautiful pedestal will only make you more aware of the offending eye-sore, but if you move the arrangement away a little, no one will notice the extinguisher! You can also camouflage ugly or plain tables by covering

them with crisp white tablecloths (well-starched sheets are a good standby if you don't own anything large enough yourself), and then placing pretty table decorations on top. In addition, you should make some large and stunning floral decorations that match the colour scheme of the wedding, not the hall! Two big arrangements are usually sufficient, and you can place them either side of the doors, next to the cake or behind the bride and groom if they will be seated. Finally, don't forget that by the time the room is filled with the wedding guests, its shortcomings won't be nearly so obvious, while your flowers will stand out marvellously.

If there is to be a receiving line, then a large arrangement nearby, consisting of subtle tones of the wedding colour scheme, will look very elegant and particularly lovely for the photographs. It will also give the guests something to look at and talk about as they wait to be received!

Working in hotels and restaurants
You can follow the same guidelines for such venues as hotels or restaurants, but you must discuss tactics with the caterers first. For instance, you won't be popular with the kitchen staff if you move into their quarters and start soaking oasis in the sinks! Most places will be able to offer you a supply of water (try the cloakrooms, if all else fails), but there may not be the space to soak the oasis and prepare the wiring, in which case you will avoid a great deal of trouble by preparing all your mechanics in advance. Then once you arrive at the venue, all you will have to do is assemble the wet oasis, cut the wire to the correct size and so on. This will also considerably help your timetable, particularly if you'll be pushed for time anyway.

Creating table decorations
Arranging flowers *in situ* is always preferable, but small table decorations are an exception. Quickly check to determine the size and shape required, then get to work at a small table to one side, out of everyone's way. This is because table decorations should be arranged sitting down—not to give you a rest (although that can be very welcome!) but because you can

DECORATING A MARQUEE BUFFET TABLE

1 *It is important to create this design in situ, because in addition to giving a better result, you may find it nigh on impossible to move the arrangement once it has been completed – it may be very heavy. Protect the table cloth as you work, preferably with some plastic sheeting placed under a large old cloth.*

2 *Assemble the mechanics. The base of the stone-coloured plastic urn is an upturned biscuit tin – it is not wise to use valuable china in a marquee, in case of accidents. Begin to build up the arrangement, keeping it simple, bold and elegant – three good principles for large designs.*

3 *The finished buffet table, with matching pedestals. Simple ribbon bows and ivy make an easy and economical garland for the table cloth.*

4 *An alternative pedestal design. Note the way in which these flowers and foliage create an entirely different atmosphere.*

SMALL TABLE DECORATIONS

1 *A flower tree makes an attractive alternative to trees made from foliage and those with added flowers. The minimum of foliage is used to cover the mechanics, and then the flowers are added to create a very luxurious feeling.*

2 *This simple basket idea is very economical, in terms of both time and money. A ribbon bow covers the handle, a painted bird sits happily on the side, and a pretty daisy plant topped with moss has been placed in a plastic-lined basket.*

3 *When making this table design it is vital that you avoid giving it the appearance of a floral pudding! This pitfall is avoided by ensuring that there is sufficient depth and recession to the design. Interesting foliage is good here as the guests will be looking at the flowers very closely. The design is created by taping a block of oasis into a plastic tray and building up the flowers around it.*

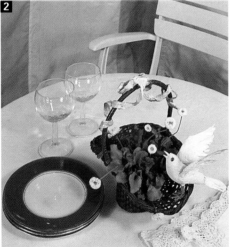

then work at the angle from which they will be viewed. Another very practical point is that creating the arrangements on the tablecloths themselves could be rather messy, and these simple shapes do not need to be viewed against their background to create the right effect.

Working in private homes

Weddings and receptions held in private homes will present different problems. The most common one is that the house is full of people, often plagued by pre-wedding nerves, and you therefore have very little space in which to work. In this case you will find it invaluable if you have prepared as much as possible in advance, and the house owners will also appreciate it if you can keep your buckets of flowers and soaking oasis in a garage or greenhouse, out of everyone's way. In the early planning stages you should have discussed your colour scheme with the bride, but may have had to compromise according to the decor of the house. For instance, pink flowers set against apricot-painted walls aren't everyone's idea of beauty! Don't forget the little touches as well as the large designs, for a simple arrangement of flowers can add a festive air to a cloakroom or bathroom.

Making the most of marquees

When a wedding is being held in a private home, a marquee or tent is often erected in the garden, and this can be great fun to decorate. Several types of marquee are available, both large and small, so you will have to adapt your designs accordingly.

For instance, a frame marquee may not have any lining, so that you will have to consider decorating all the metal supports that will be in full view. If the marquee is lined, you will have to know whether the lining will match your colour scheme, and if it has poles you will have to decide whether or not to cover or decorate them. Of course, the style of the occasion will influence your plans to a great extent, but in the main, the higher up you place the flowers, the better they will look. This is especially so if the marquee is supported by poles, because they will act as useful supports for your designs.

Trees or topiary are very suitable

Arrangements for the hall or the area in which the guests will be received are important. Many of the photographs will be taken here and the flowers add to the elegance of the occasion. As the hosts and the guests will be standing, the flowers must be arranged high up or on tall pedestals. Here, the best use has been made of the flowers while using the minimum of materials. The trails of smilax around the pedestals take the design through to the bases, thereby avoiding the fault of many pedestal designs in which the flowers appear to be perching on the top. If a larger arrangement is needed, then make sure that the foliage will flow down quite low.

because they bring the garden into the marquee, and look particularly delightful when arranged around the entrance. It is also a good idea to make a special feature of the cake table, dais or buffet table.

When planning the flowers, do remember that it can become quite warm inside a marquee, and even more so once all the guests are assembled. Heat rises, and arrangements on the top of the poles can suffer considerably as a result. It is therefore extremely important to ensure that all your oasis and moss has been thoroughly soaked, as there is no way that you will be able to water them once the ladder has been removed. A long-armed garden sprayer is useful if you want to give the flowers a last-minute misting before the guests arrive, but not everyone has one of these. If you are able to use one, do make sure that you rinse it out thoroughly before filling with water. I well remember a disastrous occasion when the sprayer had been used for weed killer and not properly washed out afterwards! You should also remember to tidy up the backs of the

If there are no tent poles, then decorating the walls of the marquee will help to give a more festive appearance. Here, linen bows, baskets of looped ivies and the minimum of flowers have been combined to create a happy design. Miniature rose bushes have been used here, making a charming present for special guests who can later plant them in their gardens or window boxes as a reminder of a lovely day.

arrangements in case it is such a warm day that the sides of the marquee are removed and your mechanics revealed!

Making two arrangements out of one
Very often a daytime reception continues with further celebrations into the evening, and one lovely way to transform your existing arrangements is to add some candles. Ideally these should be placed in candle-holders before being added to the designs, but you can make do by taping wooden toothpicks to the bases and inserting these in the oasis or wire netting. You can also buy small plastic candle holders that are then inserted into the oasis. However, you must be extremely careful with the candles, ensure that you position them sensibly and replace them each time they burn down low, otherwise they could be a perilous fire hazard. You will also have to remember to top up all the arrangements and ensure the oasis is still moist if the reception is to continue for some time.

Lavish effects on low budgets
One doesn't always have a large budget for the flowers, but there are plenty of inexpensive ideas that will still look very pretty without seeming skimped.

You can add a lot of inexpensive colour with plenty of ribbon bows, perhaps tied around the marquee poles. Garlands always look lovely but they do take time and money, so trails of smilax or ivy are a good alternative, especially if they are held up with ribbons or simple posies. Painted birds are also charming when placed in an all-green tree, perhaps with a large bow tied underneath, and look much more expensive than they really are! If your budget won't stretch to extravagant and expensive decorations on the marquee poles, wire baskets filled with variegated foliage and flowers (particularly gypsophila) can look just as lovely. To make them, soak the oasis or moss thoroughly before placing in the wire baskets, arrange the flowers and foliage and then hang in place. If you are not allowed to hammer nails into the poles, you can hang the baskets from straps or clamps instead. These may be assembled at the same time as the marquee, or put on the poles afterwards. Sometimes the pole is

DECORATING MARQUEE POLES

1 *Decorating marquee poles is fun but not always easy, and sometimes even a challenge because there are so many possibilities. Here, the mechanics have been clamped on to the pole, with wire netting encasing a block of wet oasis covered with moss.*

2 *Link the moss cages with trails of ivy and similar foliage, allowing them to drape around the pole in elegant curves.*

3 *Now add the flowers, choosing ones that enhance the colours of the marquee. Place them in the balls of mossed oasis, arranging them in such a way that they seem to be trailing down the pole with the foliage. Do not use too much decoration or the result could be overwhelming!*

covered with cloth once the lining is in position, and that could hide your clamps altogether, so try to check first.

Tidying up

As with all decorations, it will be your job to clear away your rubbish and top up the arrangements with water before the wedding or reception begins, and then remove everything afterwards. Allow plenty of time for the initial tidying up because you will be weary, and rushing around to get cleared often leads to accidents—you'll be less than thrilled if you have to re-do any of the arrangements because you've knocked them over! Once you have cleared and tidied away, give all the arrangements a quick spray of water while checking that you haven't missed anything vital, such as visible mechanics or flapping tent sides that could cause an accident. Then you can go off to work on the bouquet, corsages and posies, confident that all is well.

DECORATING THE WEDDING CAKE

1 *The cake and its decoration are an important element of any wedding. Here a little silver chalice has been arranged with wired flowers to allow a greater freedom of design.*

2 *Arrange similar flowers between the cake tiers, then place the chalice on top of the cake. The garlands of ivy around the cake table continue the decorative theme.*

CHAPTER THIRTEEN

FLORISTRY WORK

The wiring of flowers plays a very important part in floristry, and if you will be creating bouquets, posies, head dresses and the like for a wedding, you will need to know some basic floristry skills first.

Wiring flowers and foliage

Sometimes people who have a great love of flowers find it hard to accept that wiring is necessary at times. However, flowers that are to be worn or carried must be moulded into an acceptable shape, and this is where wiring comes into its own. Replacing a stem with wire enables it to be coaxed into a shape that can then be used as part of a posy, bouquet, corsage, buttonhole or head dress—something that would never be possible with the natural stem of the flower.

It goes without saying that the wires must be as inconspicuous as possible, and the finished work lightweight and comfortable to wear and hold. There are many gauges of wire available, but one should always choose the finest gauge that will hold the flower firmly in position. The greatest care should also be taken when handling the flowers and foliage because they can easily be bruised through rough treatment.

The types of wire

The wires used for most spray work are sold as stub wires in the standard imperial wire gauges of 20, 22 and 24. (The higher the number, the finer the gauge.) These numberings are gradually being replaced by metric measurements, in which case they are sold as 0.90mm, 0.71mm and 0.56mm respectively, and the rule is that the *lower* the number, the finer the wire! You may find this difficult to remember at first but you should soon adjust.

Silver wire is available in reels of varying

A bouquet and head dress of lilies laid out ready for the bride.

MAKING A
CORSAGE

1 *Wire and then tape the individual flowers and foliage.*

2 *Build up the shape of the corsage, taping the flowers together.*

3 *When the corsage is completed, tape the stem tightly then finish off neatly. Make sure you attach a safety pin to the corsage ready for wearing.*

thicknesses, and also in lengths of approximately 180mm (7in). It is often much easier and quicker to work with these cut lengths, and 0.38mm (28 gauge) and 0.28mm (32 gauge) wires are the most useful sizes. For convenience, and to avoid confusion when you are busy, keep each gauge of stub wire in a different, clearly marked, container that will stand up properly. It is essential to store the wires in a dry place to prevent them rusting—a rusty stub wire will stain first your hands and then the plant material quite disastrously. Nevertheless, a rusting wire can be used to advantage in floristry, because when a wire comes into contact with the sap of the stem it will soon go rusty, therefore holding the stem and the wire together very securely. However, this will not happen until the stem has been taped.

Stem tapes
These are used to cover wires and are available in several colours and quantities. One of the most popular on the market is a slightly sticky tape which the novice will find easier to hold than the rubbery gutta percha, which is used most often. The sticky tape also keeps better—gutta percha just crumbles away after a time. Unfortunately the tape is only sold in one width and very often narrower gutta percha is preferable, especially when using silver wires for such floristry work as corsages and head dresses.

The tape is usually cut in half by hand, but this is a very laborious task. Help is at hand, however, in cake decorating shops! Sugarpaste flowers require extremely narrow stem tape for their very fine stems, for which you can buy a three-bladed stem cutter. This will also solve your problem with the sticky tape. Remove the two outer blades, leaving just the central one, and you will be able to cut tape to the exact size for covering silver wire stems for spray work. I think that the time and effort saved by this little gadget more than justifies its inclusion in any list of floristry equipment.

Ribbons often provide the perfect finishing touch, and some paper ribbons are widely used. However, real ribbon is always preferable to me, as it is available in

so many lovely colours, widths and qualities. It may be expensive but I believe that the difference it makes to the end result is worth the extra expense. In fact, a lesson you will quickly learn about floristry is that you get the best results only by using the best material available, thereby enabling you to produce work of which you can be justly proud.

Spray work
Here is a list of flowers and foliage that can be successfully wired for spray work:

Alchemilla	Lily
Alstroemeria	Lily of the valley
Cyclamen	Nigella
Carnation	Orchid
Erica	Pittosporum
Eucalyptus	Ranunculus
Euonymus	Rhododendron
Freesia	Rose
Geranium	Senecio
Gladiolus	Spray carnation
Hedera	Stephanotis
Helleborus	Tradescantia
Hyacinth pips	

Before using either flowers or foliage, it is important that both have been properly conditioned (*see pp. 10–14*) to improve both their appearance and performance. Remember that once the plant material has been wired it will not be in water or oasis, and will have to stay looking good for at least a day. Conditioning for several hours is therefore necessary, during which time the material should be kept in as cool a place as possible (but not the fridge). The flowers will be crisp and firm but quite brittle, and their stems will tend to snap more easily (more often than not in the wrong place!), so handle them as carefully as you can.

If you will be picking your material from the garden, then do so preferably early in the morning or late in the evening. Take a bucket, half-filled with water, into the garden with you and place each flower or piece of foliage in it immediately after

To wire an ivy leaf, keep the back of the leaf
uppermost and, about three-quarters of the way
up the leaf, push a wire through it to make a tiny
'stitch'. Move the wire until there are two equal
legs, then bend them downwards. Make one lie
against the stem and twist the other leg around
the stem and the wire, thus holding it in place.
Then bind this wire and stem with stem tape.

To wire a single Singapore orchid, detach it
from its stem then push a wire through the base
of the flower head, keeping one leg of wire much
shorter than the other, and twist the longer
wire around the shorter one. Bind with stem
tape. To make a spray, wire up each orchid
individually then tape them together.

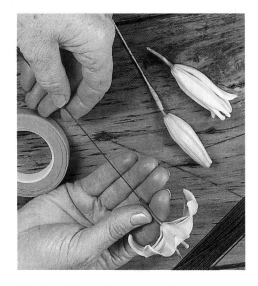

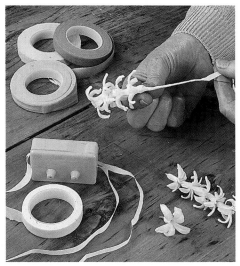

To wire a lily, cut off the stem until about
2.5cm (1in) remains, then carefully push a
thick wire up the stem, and bind tightly with
stem tape.

Hyacinth pips can be wired together to form a
spray that adds interest to a bouquet. Bend
over the top of a wire to form a crook, then push
it down through the pip until the wire loop is
hidden. Now push further pips up the wire and
bind the remaining wire stem with stem tape.

MAKING A BUTTONHOLE

1 *Cut out a small circle of card and make a small cut in the centre. Remove the outer leaves and seed pod of the carnation but leave the stem intact.*

2 *Push the card circle into place as shown, then feed the wire through the back of the carnation. Wire up some ivy leaves.*

3 *Neatly tape the leaves and carnation together. The buttonhole is now ready for use. It will look very elegant and sit easily in a buttonhole.*

WIRING A ROSE

1 *Push a thick wire up the stem of the rose, then push two wires through the base of the petals at 90° to each other.*

2 *Twist the wires down the stems, then bind with stem tape. To make a spray, tape one rose into the stem of the next.*

cutting. This will ensure the plant material has no chance to droop.

It is very important to choose mature leaves for floristry, since using young foliage will be courting disaster—the material will bruise very easily and probably disintegrate when wired. It is a waste to pick and condition plant material that cannot be used, and far better to leave it on the plant for future use.

The flowers I have mentioned are the more usual ones chosen for spray work, but don't be afraid to experiment with other flowers too. Not, I hasten to add, on the day itself, but try out the proposed materials a few days before the event and if your experiment is successful you can carry on. If not, then you will have time to review the situation and find a more suitable alternative. It is only by experimenting that discoveries are made, so don't be hidebound!

Technical floristry terms
Like any other trade, the floristry business has several technical terms to explain various techniques and items. Here is a list of the most frequently used terms, and their explanations. Familiarising yourself with each one will prove very useful.
Binding—this uses silver reel wire to hold the leaves and wires in place.
Guttaring—the process by which the wires are covered with tape. As well as the eponymous gutta percha, other sorts of tape are also available.
Leg mounts—the wires that are attached to the flower, pips, etc. They vary, having double, single, extended and even false legs. The latter is used when the wire replaces or extends the stem.
Pips—individual flowers taken from a flower such as a hyacinth.
Spray or corsage—an arrangement of flowers worn on the shoulder of a coat or dress.
Stitching leaves—the process of wiring leaves.
Wiring down—inserting the wire into the head of the flower and then wiring on the inside or outside of the stem for support.

The step-by-step photographs clearly show how to wire individual flowers, and also

FEATHERING CARNATIONS

1 Carefully separate a few petals from the main flower then wire the bases of their petals together, twisting the wire downwards as shown in the photograph.

To wire a carnation, cut off its stem until no more than 2.5cm (1in) remains, then push a wire through the base of the flower head as shown, leaving one leg much shorter than the other. Bind the stem and wire with stem tape.

2 Bind the wire with stem tape to give small, delicate flowers that are ideal for use in bouquets and head dresses.

To wire a spray of lily of the valley, wind a length of wire between the bells, then pull it down the stem and bind firmly in place with stem tape.

MAKING A BOUQUET

1 *Wire and tape the large ivy leaves and roses, then tape them into the design, making the combined stems the handle of the bouquet.*

2 *Tie a length of ribbon into a large bow just below the foliage so that it will be visible when the bouquet is carried.*

MAKING A LARGE LOOSE HEAD DRESS

1 *Wire and tape all the individual roses and foliage.*

2 *Begin to tape the flowers and foliage into the design, binding all the stems very tightly as you work.*

3 *Finish off the tape when you have completed the head dress, ensuring that all the wires have been covered.*

illustrate how each type of stem is wired. Once you have mastered these techniques, you will able to follow any of the instructions for wired wedding designs.

You will soon see how useful the wired stems are when creating differing styles. Every bride-to-be has her own ideas about her wedding flowers and it is important to discover these before rushing into a particular style. The cut, colour and style of her wedding outfit will also play a large part in your final floral design.

Arrangements in the hair

Flowers in the hair are always very attractive and are once again enjoying a revival in popularity. There are several styles that can be considered, and the four that are illustrated here should give you plenty of ideas for further shapes and designs. However intricate or beautiful your design, do remember that it must be comfortable for the wearer, and will have to be firmly secured in place.

Bouquets and posies

The bouquet is always a focal point of a wedding, and usually causes quite a stir. I will always remember the sensation created by the Princess of Wales with her beautiful bouquet. It contained so many flowers that it must have been quite heavy to carry. One of my favourite bouquets of all is a simple sheaf of lilies, which is elegant and beautiful.

The six designs illustrated here should once again inspire you to create ideas of your own. The posy, hoop and basket are perfect for little bridesmaids or the flower girl, and the rather more adult styles are ideal for the older bridesmaids, matron of honour and the bride herself.

It goes without saying that you should use beautiful materials, and you will create a more interesting design if you can introduce one or two surprises. For instance, variegated ivy is very pretty, and individually wired leaves can be made into sprays that give a delicate touch and lighten the design. Nevertheless, it is important to choose suitable flowers for the particular style. For example, some carefully arranged gypsophila is delightful when used in flowers for children, but don't use too much or it will envelop everything else!

MAKING A LOOSE BOUQUET

1 *Wire and tape all the roses, ivy and other plant material ready to be incorporated into the design. Then place the flowers in a container of oasis to prevent damaging the blooms and making it easy to select the material needed.*

2 *Begin to create the basic shape with the foliage. The handle will be created by taping the wires from each 'stem'.*

3 *Now add the roses, taping each one in place as you work. These 'Champagne' roses help to create a delicate, elegant and flowing design, that is accentuated when lovely and interesting foliage is used.*

4 *Once you have finished making the bouquet, make sure its handle is securely bound with tape. You can then leave it as it is (although it may be rather sticky unless you have used gutta percha) or bind it with a decorative ribbon.*

5 *The finished bouquet. This design beautifully complements the deep oyster silk of the dress.*

MAKING A FRONTAL HEAD DRESS

1 *Wire and tape each lily ready for use.*

2 *Beginning the design with the buds and half-opened lilies, tape the stems together, working in the foliage as the design is created.*

3 *Once the head dress is the correct size for the wearer, finish binding the wires with stem tape, but do ensure that no sharp or uncomfortable ends of wires are sticking out.*

Other ideas for young bridesmaids

If you're looking for something different, a flower ball is a very pretty idea. It is easily made, using a mossed ball as a base, into which small and pretty wired flowers are inserted until every piece of moss is covered and the flower ball is a perfect sphere. Then a simple bow and loop should be securely pinned into the finished ball so that it can be carried in the hand. Don't make the flower ball too large or it will look somewhat clumsy and cumbersome.

A prayer book spray is another pleasing idea and is easy to carry. The spray should not be too large and is stitched on to a piece of pretty ribbon so that it can be used as a book marker. You can also wire and stitch some very small pips and foliage to the ends of the ribbons for added interest. Stitching the ribbon lightly where the piece is folded back will keep the design firm, but remember to fold the ribbon with the right side showing.

Transporting the wedding flowers

Before you begin to arrange or wire the flowers you must consider how you are going to transport the finished bouquets, posies, buttonholes and other wedding flowers to their destination. They may have to travel quite a distance, so you will have to protect them as much as possible to ensure that they arrive in pristine condition.

Large flower boxes are marvellous. Although the smart white ones may look more elegant, it really doesn't matter what colour the box is as long as you have paid proper attention to its inside. The box will be discarded, anyway! Line the box with a layer of fine polythene and then tissue paper. In this case, white is the best colour, because not only will there be no danger of the colour bleeding on to the flowers, but it will also look immaculate—a beautifully set out box will give great pleasure. Crumple the tissue paper to form a shock-absorbent base on which you can place the designs. If there are any ribbon bows, tuck a little crumpled tissue paper into the bows themselves to keep them rounded and uncreased. If ends of the ribbons are to trail, arrange them on the tissue to ensure that they will not be creased.

Even short journeys can be bumpy, so it

MAKING A WEDDING SHEAF

1 *A wedding sheaf is essentially a design in which beautiful, simple flowers are tied into a bouquet, giving the appearance that it has just been gathered from the garden. This is not a difficult design to make but it does require care and attention to detail. Not every flower is suitable for this design, as very fragile flowers will be broken long before the wedding. Lilies are an ideal choice.*

2 *Strip the lower stems of their foliage, then assemble the flowers together so that they look attractive. Bind the stems together with soft green garden twine.*

3 *Tie off the twine, then camouflage it with a large handsome ribbon. The bouquet is shown here with its matching head dress* (see facing page*).*

It is essential to pack any wedding flowers properly if they will be transported from one place to another. Here, the coronet and two corsages have been placed in a box on a bed of crumpled tissue paper to protect the flowers. They are then given a very fine misting of water – do not use too much or you may spoil the appearance of the flowers.

Flowers can be used singly or in sprays to decorate hair, and woven or pinned into position. Here, lilies have been incorporated into a plait for a simple but elegant look.

is a good idea to tie the contents into the box. Thread a large needle with some thick thread, then push it through the base of the box, over the handle or centre of the design, and then back underneath before securing. For extra security, it is a good idea to repeat the process further down the box. If some of the flowers are a little heavy, you can support their undersides with a little crumpled tissue paper. Once you are confident that your designs are properly protected and supported, spray the flowers with a fine mist of water, cover with a few sheets of tissue paper followed by another layer of polythene and then replace the lid, having first checked that there is ample space for you to do so!

It is a very good idea to place a warning note on top of the polythene sheet, giving

simple removal instructions—otherwise an unwary bride or her mother could well damage the contents of the box by trying to pull out flowers that have been firmly anchored in place. You could also include in this note instructions to keep the box cool and undisturbed until required. (That probably won't prevent the recipient having a quick look to see what you've done, though!) Another useful tip is to write 'This side up' on the sides and lid to avoid accidents. 'Better safe than sorry' is definitely the motto to remember here!

Follow these simple instructions, and you'll be confident that you've done your utmost to ensure that the wedding flowers look their very best and help to make the day a truly unforgettable occasion.

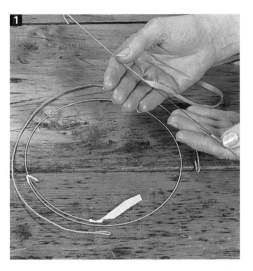

MAKING A FLOWER CORONET

1 *Measure the head of the girl who will wear the coronet, then cut a piece of wire to this size, but allowing a little extra at each end. Bind the wire with stem tape, then bend the wire back on itself at each end at the correct point to form a hook and eye. Millinery wire is preferable as it already has the rounded shape needed.*

2 *Wire and tape the individual flowers and foliage along the taped wire.*

3 *Complete the coronet. Here, it is shown resting on a veil.*

4 *You can make small versions of the coronet for young bridesmaids, adding some ribbons if required.*

MAKING A
FLOWER HOOP

1 *Bind the hoop with ribbon. Make a long garland of small and delicate wired flowers and foliage, taping them together.*

2 *Gently twist the garland around the hoop and wire it in place. Hide the join with a large ribbon bow.*

This is an alternative flower hoop. It has been left unbound and only a few flowers have been wired in place before being decorated with ribbon bows.

MAKING A BRIDESMAID'S CIRCLET AND BASKET

1 *Make a circlet in the same way as you would a flower coronet (see pp. 138–9), but split the stem tape in half for a more delicate finish. You can also make a long garland in the same way, which can then be carried by two small bridesmaids, or tied to their wrists for easy carrying.*

2 *Prepare the basket by lining it with plastic and wire a piece of wet oasis into the bottom. You can also use a frog for extra stability.*

3 *Add the flowers and foliage, arranging it to hide the mechanics and sit neatly in the basket without obscuring the handle, by which it will be carried. This soft flowing design will not be easily damaged – young bridesmaids can be very active!*

4 *The finished circlet and basket, worn by a young bridesmaid.*

CONDITIONING TIPS FOR FLOWERS AND FOLIAGE

Many flowers and foliage can be conditioned in the ordinary way, but this is a list of the plant material that needs extra care if it is to look at its best when arranged. If you will be picking the plant material yourself, you will gain the best results if you gather flowers and foliage either early or late in the day. After soaking the plant material, allow it to drain on newspaper before arranging.

Alchemilla mollis	Normal conditioning. Cut stems under water if desired.
Alstroemeria	Normal conditioning. Cut stems under water if desired.
Althaea (hollyhock)	Dip ends in boiling water. Give long drink in deep water.
Anemone	Dip ends in boiling water. Give cool drink. Prefer water to oasis.
Astrantia	Normal conditioning. Cut stems under water if desired.
Azalea	Hammer woody stems. Scrape bark back a little. Give long drink.
Begonia rex	Dip stems in boiling water for 30 seconds then submerge in cold water. Dry and use with as much stem in the water as possible.
Bergenia	Submerge in water.
Camellia	Hammer stem ends. Give long drink.
Chaenomeles	Hammer stem ends. Give long drink.
Choisya ternata	Hammer stem ends. Give long drink.
Chrysanthemum (all-year-round)	Normal conditioning. Cut stems under water if desired.
Clematis vitalba (old man's beard)	Dip stems in boiling water. Give long drink. Does well when leaves are glycerined.
Cobaea scandens	Normal conditioning. Cut stems under water if desired.
Corylopsis	Hammer stem ends. Give long drink.
Delphinium	Fill hollow stems with water then plug with cotton wool. Give long drink.
Dianthus (carnation)	Cut above or below joints on stems. Give long drink.
Dicentra spectabilis	Give drink of warm water.
Digitalis (foxglove)	Give drink of warm water.
Elaeagnus	Hammer stem ends. Give long drink.
Eremurus	Normal conditioning. Cut stems under water if desired.
Eucalyptus	Normal conditioning. Cut stems under water if desired.
Euphorbia	Scald or burn stem ends. Give long drink. Take care when handling the stems as their milky sap is a strong irritant.
Fatsia	Normal conditioning. Cut stems under water if desired.
Forsythia	Hammer stem ends. Give long drink. Does well if forced for early flowering.
Garrya elliptica	Hammer stem ends. Give long drink.
Gladiolus	Normal conditioning. Cut stems under water if desired.
Hedera (ivy)	Soak in water.
Helleborus	Dip stems in boiling water. Give long drink. Prick below head.
Hosta	Soak in water.
Hydrangea	Dip stems in boiling water. Submerge whole stem, including head, for an hour or two.
Laurus (laurel)	Soak in water.
Ligustrum (privet)	Hammer stem ends. Give long drink.

Lilium (lily)	Give long drink. Remove the stamens as their pollen can stain.
Malus (crab apple)	Hammer stem ends. Give long drink.
Matthiola (stock)	Strip foliage below water line.
Moluccella	Normal conditioning. Cut stems under water if desired.
Myrsiphyllum asparagoides (smilax)	Normal conditioning. Cut stems under water if desired.
Neillia	Hammer stem ends. Give long drink.
Nicotiana (tobacco plant)	Give drink of warm water.
Ornamental cabbage and kale	Normal conditioning. Cut stems under water if desired.
Paeonia (peony)	Normal conditioning. Cut stems under water if desired.
Papaver (poppy)	Pick when the colour is just showing in the bud. Burn stem ends. Give long drink.
Philadelphus (mock orange)	Remove most or all of leaves. Hammer stem ends. Give long drink.
Phormium tenax	Normal conditioning. Cut stems under water if desired.
Physocarpus opulifolius	Hammer stem ends. Give long drink.
Polygonatum (Solomon's seal)	Normal conditioning. Cut stems under water if desired.
Prunus	Hammer stem ends. Give long drink.
Rhododendron	Hammer stem ends. Give long drink.
Ribes (flowering currant)	Hammer stem ends. Give long drink. Forces well for early flowering.
Rosa (rose)	Dip stems in boiling water. Give long cool drink.
Sorbus aria (whitebeam)	Hammer stem ends. Give long cool drink.
Spirea × arguta (bridal wreath)	Hammer stem ends. Give long cool drink.
Stachyurus praecox	Hammer stem ends. Give long drink.
Symphoricarpos (snowberry)	Use the berries. Strip the leaves.
Syringa (lilac)	Hammer stem ends. Give long drink. Remove all foliage.
Tellima grandiflora	Dip stems in boiling water. Give long cool drink.
Tiarella	Soak the leaves.
Tulipa (tulip)	Prick stem below the head with a fine needle. Wrap in newspaper and give a cool drink.
Viburnum	Hammer stems. Give long drink.
Vinca	Dip ends in boiling water. Submerge in cold water.
Weigela	Hammer stems. Give long drink.
Zantedeschia aethiopica (Arum lily)	Give long drink up to neck. Submerge leaves.
Zinnias	Give long drink.